FOX CITIES MURDER & MAYHEM

FOX CITIES MURDER & MAYHEM

GAVIN SCHMITT

THE History PRESS

Published by The History Press
Charleston, SC
www.historypress.net

Front cover, top: Lyle Hansen; *bottom*: author's collection.
Back cover, top: Neenah Public Library; *bottom*: Kaukauna Public Library.

First published 2017

Manufactured in the United States

ISBN 9781467138697

Library of Congress Control Number: 2017948492

CONTENTS

ACKNOWLEDGEMENTS

Thank you to The History Press, for taking a chance on me. One only hopes you made the right decision. Thank you, also, to the readers who have kept me on this path the last several years. Really, the hustle of the "author life" has been living the dream. I can't thank you all enough.

Some stories in this book were originally developed by myself twenty years ago but never published until now. Thank you to the librarians who allowed me all the endless hours on the microfilm reader in the years before most of the articles were available online. Also, thanks to the anonymous diligent reporters (long since dead) who provided the source material.

When compiling this book, a few people came forward with new stories I had not previously known about. I was pointed toward the George Hammer case early on. The Blazing Stump has been a research request from readers for a few years now. How I first heard of the Appleton Butcher I don't recall, but I'm sure it was from someone who knew the incident would spark my interest.

Last, but not least, thanks to my brother Andy, whose love of history enriches my own. Over and over again, he has had me look into things I didn't even know I was interested in. Vice is my wheelhouse, but he's invited me into his (local breweries). Every now and then, the two collide.

A NOTE ON SOURCES

The stories covered in *Fox Cities Murder & Mayhem* have not appeared in any previous publication to my knowledge. Therefore, the source material is primarily newspaper articles written by uncredited journalists in Appleton, Kaukauna, Neenah and beyond. The stories were fleshed out through the use of biographical and genealogical sources: census records, death certificates, military draft registrations and so on.

In addition, some of the material in the chapter on Frances Webb comes from the parole files of Fred Runde, which are available from the State Historical Society of Wisconsin. Special thanks to Jane Lang and the Neenah Historical Society for providing a copy of these records and saving me a trip to Madison.

Lastly, while the skeleton of the Appleton Butcher story is from news reports filed by Bill Knudson, the real flesh of the story comes from the police report itself. My thanks to Mary Schmeichel and the Appleton Police Department for providing me with a copy. Despite some minor redactions for the protection of medical privacy, the document was a wealth of information and a genuine page-turner.

INTRODUCTION

I know what you must be thinking on picking up this book for the first time: the Fox Cities are not known for their "murder and mayhem." And you're absolutely right. For the most part, the series of small towns that make up the region are some of the safest places in America and great places to raise a family. So, why does this book exist?

Beyond my own interest in "dark history," I think the book offers a look at the community in a way we rarely think of it. We aren't aware that brothels were common and operated more or less on an open basis, free from police interference. We think of the past as "the good old days," but some of the most sensational crimes in local history took place long ago, not last week. And who knew that the Chinese community was thriving (albeit small) in various cities throughout northeast Wisconsin before the 1900s?

Now these stories will be told, for the first time in book form and in greater detail than newspapers allowed. History is history, whether good or bad. Rather than romanticize the past and build up our ancestors into untouchable idols, let us instead embrace the far more interesting truth. Humanity has always been populated by imperfect miscreants—and always will be.

One final thought: part of what makes a hero is a villain to overcome. Although the focus here may be on the villains, let us not overlook the unsung heroes in each story—the police, the judges and even the newspapermen who shone light into the shadows.

1
THE INTEMPERATE MURDER OF MAGDALENA HESSE

Our first story is one of crumbling marital relationships and the thriving temperance movement in Neenah during the 1870s. Whether or not alcohol was entirely to blame, the "demon drink" was certainly a factor in the lives of the Hesse family.

Magdalena Friese Hesse was born in Hanover, Germany, around 1834 and came to the United States around 1849. Some time was spent in both New York and Boston; in the former, she married and had two children, but this attempt at a family was a tragic affair. Both children died young, and her husband was a drunkard, leading to a quick divorce. Possibly through shame, despair or regret, he hanged himself within months of her leaving. While in Boston, Magdalena boarded with a wealthy family and essentially worked as a domestic. She was praised for her attention to detail. Wanderlust was within her, and Magdalena ultimately settled in Neenah around 1860.

Within a year of her removal to Neenah, Magdalena met young John Hesse, nine years her junior. He lived with his parents and siblings in a home much too small for everyone. Henry Hesse, his father, did his best to support the family on his salary as a butcher, and mother Henrietta Alles Hesse took care of her husband and seven children. John was a man of dark complexion, with black hair and dark eyes, and had a "most villainous cast of countenance" when under the influence of alcohol. He had been born in Germany and came with his parents from Crivitz in Mecklenburg–West Pomerania. (Crivitz in Wisconsin is named for the German city.)

The marriage of John and Magdalena produced seven children, though two died before reaching maturity. For John, the marriage was a step up in society. Magdalena was the owner of farmland valued at $6,000, far more than anything his parents had to offer. And, given the social mores of the day, although the farm was "hers," the property was now controlled by him.

In 1864, the family was proudly part of the Presbyterian Church, and on one occasion, John even loaned the princely sum of $800 to a local minister with the full knowledge that he might never get it back. Though the Hesse family was not known to be more committed to their religion than the average citizen, two of John's sisters married Huelster brothers. The Huelsters were elders in the church near Lomira. Anton Huelster earned a doctorate and served as a professor of theology. Unexpected by everyone, John was forcefully ejected from the congregation when he turned to alcohol. He grew to be a terror to his family and friends. Magdalena was allowed to continue her church attendance, but John was forbidden, and the church elders strongly encouraged a divorce. Soon enough, she agreed.

Throughout 1869 and 1870, John Hesse was becoming a nuisance not only to his family but also to the community at large. He was engaged in what the newspapers termed "debauchery" and was known to lock his children outside at night. On at least one occasion, he threatened Magdalena with a butcher knife. According to the press, "His inordinate passion for liquor has made him a brute." The city was "outraged and insulted" by Hesse and other "lawless creatures crazed with bad whiskey."

During one court incident in 1869, defense attorney Elbridge Smith asked the judge if he could speak to Hesse in private. The judge agreed, and the two stepped out the back door. When Smith came back in, the judge asked him where Hesse had gone. Smith allegedly replied, "I advised my client that his case was hopeless and the best thing he could do was to run." The newspaper makes no mention of the attorney being reprimanded for this stunt, an action that could rightly have gotten him disbarred. Smith, incidentally, was Neenah's first attorney, having passed the bar as early as 1849.

On January 1, 1871, Hesse was accused by his recently divorced wife of entering her home and assaulting her with a deadly weapon. He was arrested by a marshal named Ellis and brought before Justice Chester C. Townsend. Hesse was immediately transported to the county jail in order to allow him a few days to "sober off." Some confusion at the jail allowed Hesse to go free, and he roamed the streets of Oshkosh for a few days.

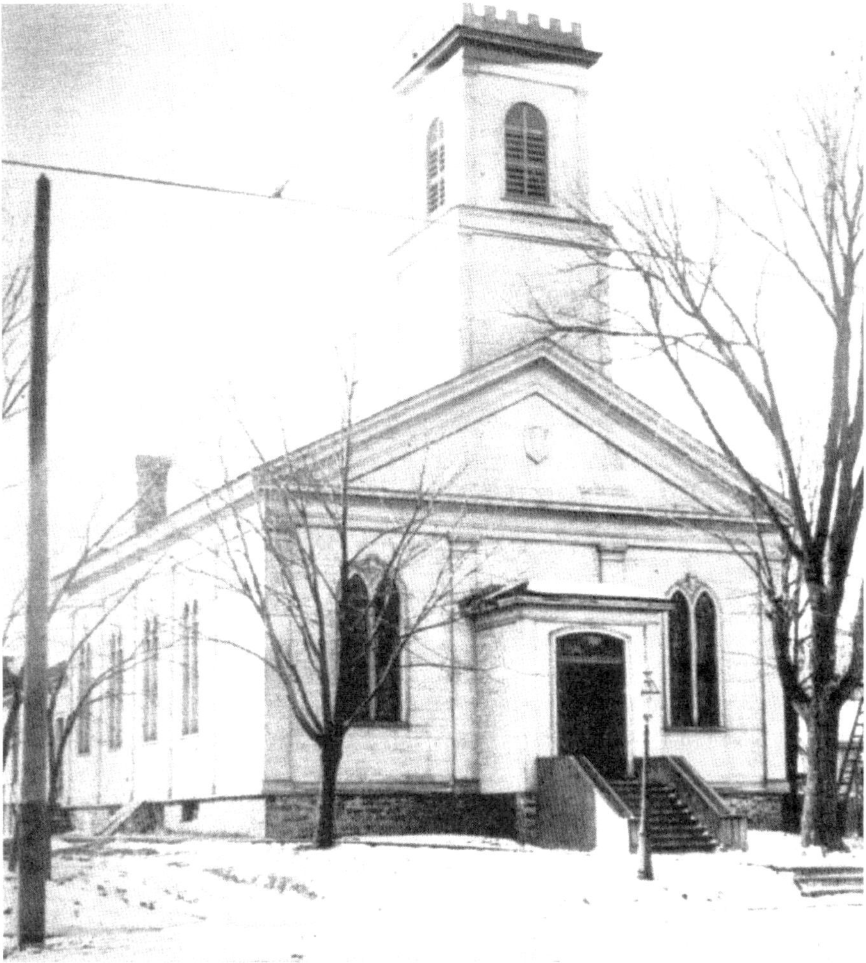

The First Presbyterian Church in Neenah, most likely the church attended by the Hesse family. *Neenah Historical Society*.

Within the week, he was back at his ex-wife's door, this time pleading his love to her and asking for reconciliation. She politely declined, and he became a bit more forceful, demanding her to make him dinner while he took a nap in her bed. Sheriff Ephraim Giddings, a Civil War captain in the Third Wisconsin Infantry, was called. Hesse was again brought before Justice Townsend, who charged him with breaking the peace and issued a bond of $800. Not having the money, Hesse was personally brought by Giddings on the evening train to Oshkosh and locked up under the watch of young Sheriff Ambrose H. Woodworth, only twenty-one years

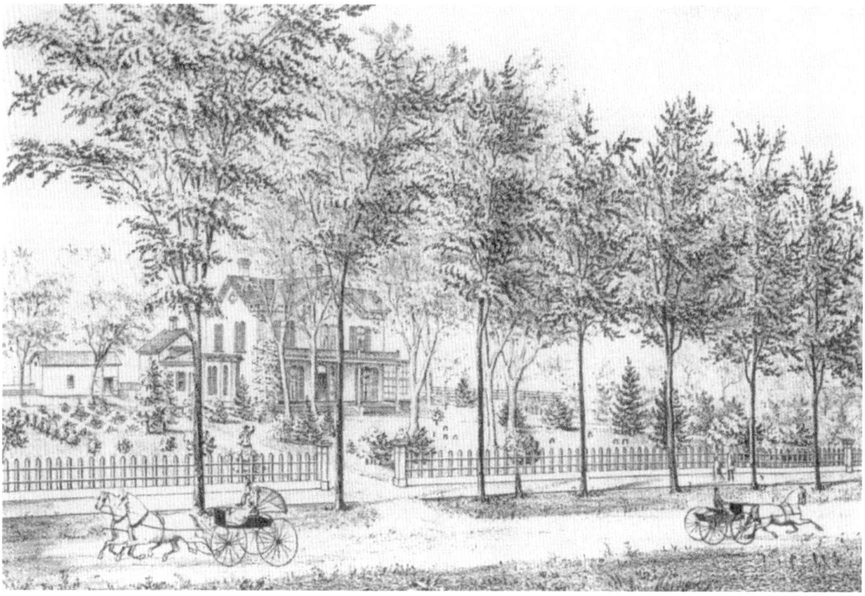

The home of Elbridge Smith, one of the earliest attorneys of the Neenah-Menasha area. *Menasha Historical Society.*

old. Giddings warned Woodworth that Hesse was vicious and seemed to be getting worse every day.

The local newspaper editorialized on January 7, "This community have felt themselves outraged and insulted of late, by a set of lawless creatures, crazed with bad whiskey, who for some reason have been allowed to pursue their own course, unmolested by officers, whom the public look to for protection from such outrages." While this suggested that multiple offenders were making a drunken scene about town, their singling out of Hesse could not have been more prescient.

By February 24, Hesse had sobered up and, according to Woodworth, began to act like a total gentleman, admitting to his bad behavior and taking the blame on himself. He further said that he could not control himself when under the power of whiskey. Woodworth felt that Hesse's repentance was "sincere." Jailer O.P. White was given fifty dollars by Hesse to put in the bank for his family and another thirty dollars for White to hold on to for anything Hesse might need while in jail. By sheer coincidence, that same day, the door was left open and unattended between one and two o'clock in the afternoon, allowing Hesse to slip out unnoticed. The sheriff had business to attend to in his hometown of Omro and was not around. Woodworth later testified that it "may look to many like carelessness or culpable negligence on my part," but he swore that no desire to let Hesse escape was intended. In his defense, he noted that Hesse had to break through a padlock, which in hindsight was clearly not strong enough. Another prisoner, a man named Wilson, later said the security was routinely very lax in the jail, with visitors often handed keys in order to visit their loved ones. Wilson himself had more or less a run of the jail, as he did odd jobs around the place such as bringing wood inside for the kitchen stove. Wilson even claimed that when the sheriff noticed Hesse was gone, he did not seem "anxious or uneasy."

That night and the following day, John stayed with his elder brother Julius and sister-in-law Lena. In later testimony, Lena admitted that John had actually told them how much he wanted to kill his ex-wife, but when he left them on the evening of February 25, he said he was done with her and was moving to California. In fact, he went instead to the tavern of August Melchert, where he drank with his friend, English-born mason Mathew Loomis, for two hours and urged his brother Julius to give him a revolver in case he had to fight off the police. Julius initially agreed, hoping to help his brother avoid arrest, and purchased such a weapon from gunsmith Hiram Harder for fifteen dollars. Julius ultimately changed his mind about helping John, however, when he stopped at home and Lena told him what the revolver was really for.

After years of threatening, John finally killed his ex-wife on February 25 in her own home, some time after nine o'clock that evening. Magdalena was held down, and with a knife, Hesse slashed her neck, severing her carotid artery and jugular—a quick and bloody demise. She was thirty-seven. All five children, ages thirteen months through nine years, were in the home at the time. Amazingly, none of the children was woken during the crime. Franklin, the eldest, found his mother at daybreak and immediately ran to the nearby home of Gorham Parsons Vining to get help. When Dr. Samuel Galentine was eventually called to the house, he found her lying on her back, near the stove. He later testified that the wound was so deep and violent that there was simply no way the injury could have been self-inflicted or accidental. Dr. George Washington Fay and a Dr. Potter assisted in the postmortem and concurred with the initial findings.

After the murder, John had gone to William Hesse's hotel within the village limits and hid out in an attic or garret. Unfortunately for him, he was seen by no less a citizen than Charles Benjamin Clark, who would become best known as the cofounder of Kimberly-Clark the following year. Clark saw Hesse crossing the street from the Pettibone Block to the Hesse

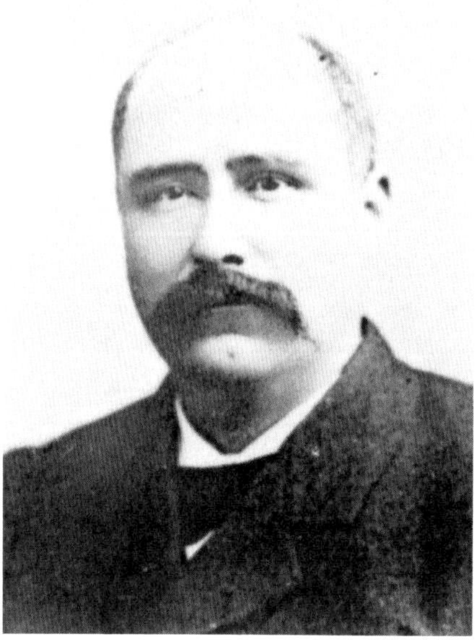

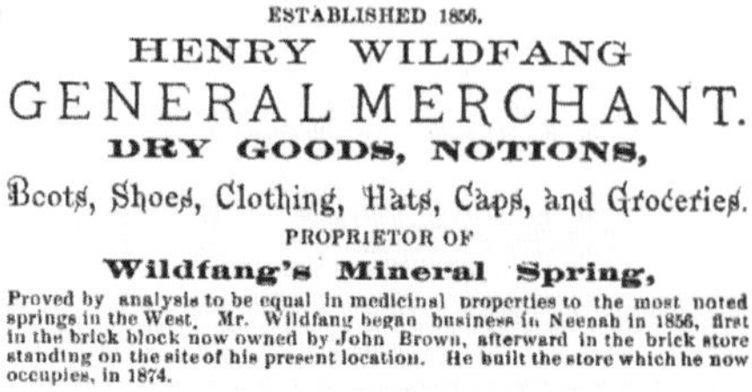

ESTABLISHED 1856.

HENRY WILDFANG

GENERAL MERCHANT.

DRY GOODS, NOTIONS,

Boots, Shoes, Clothing, Hats, Caps, and Groceries.

PROPRIETOR OF

Wildfang's Mineral Spring,

Proved by analysis to be equal in medicinal properties to the most noted springs in the West. Mr. Wildfang began business in Neenah in 1856, first in the brick block now owned by John Brown, afterward in the brick store standing on the site of his present location. He built the store which he now occupies, in 1874.

Above: An ad for the business of Henry Wildfang, brother-in-law to the Hesse family. *Author's collection.*

Left: C.B. Clark, the cofounder of Kimberly-Clark in Neenah. *Neenah Historical Society.*

Hotel and alerted a Mr. Holdbrook, telling him to get Sheriff Giddings. Clark, like Giddings, had been an infantry captain during the war. With a Mr. Whiting, a Mr. Williams, Isaac L. "Ike" Doton and William N. Conover, Clark surrounded the hotel until Giddings arrived. Inside was Henry Robinson, who said he had been there when John Hesse arrived and claimed that Hesse confessed to the murder, said he was glad that he did the deed and further wished he had killed his brother-in-law Henry Wildfang while he was at it, too.

Sheriff Giddings gathered a posse of local men and entered the hotel of William Hesse. While there, John apparently realized that his freedom was at an end and fired two shots from the attic. At least one struck himself and was fatal. With a makeshift spear provided by Conover, Giddings broke a hole in the ceiling and found the lifeless body of John Hesse in the attic. He had shot himself in the forehead, just above the bridge of his nose. William Hesse allowed Giddings to stay and finish his work but kindly asked the posse to return to their homes. Doton and Conover lowered the body to the ground with a rope and rested it on a bench.

On February 27, Henry Wildfang, falsely identified by the newspapers as Magdalena Hesse's brother-in-law, filed a claim in probate court, as Magdalena had died intestate and the farm property was in her name. With her husband also deceased and the children so young, a proper disposal of the real estate was needed. Wildfang was, in fact, John Hesse's brother-in-law, having been married to his sister Louisa. Magdalena's sister, Caroline Minck, came to town from Philadelphia to see to the welfare of the children.

Gathering at the Hesse home, Justice of the Peace James Conlon conducted an inquest on February 28, calling all those involved. His jury consisted of farmer Albert Huxley, supervisor Henry E. Huxley, brickmaker Jerome Bailey, John W. Halstead, Gorham Parsons Vining and David Wells. Their verdict, not surprisingly, was murder. Vining, interestingly, was the brother-in-law of Henry Huxley and one of Neenah's oldest citizens, having operated the government mill when the village was still known as Winnebago Rapids.

On March 4, funerals were held for both John Hesse and his ex-wife. Hesse's father attended both services, and it was said that John was buried "near the slough." The city paid J. Brennan five dollars for his services in digging the Hesse grave. Presumably, the grave has since been moved, as the slough is surrounded by houses today. Where John lies now is not known. Immediately following the burial, Dr. Christian Linde of Oshkosh filed a request to have the body exhumed for the purpose of dissection and to advance the interests of science. Despite being the oldest physician in Winnebago County and

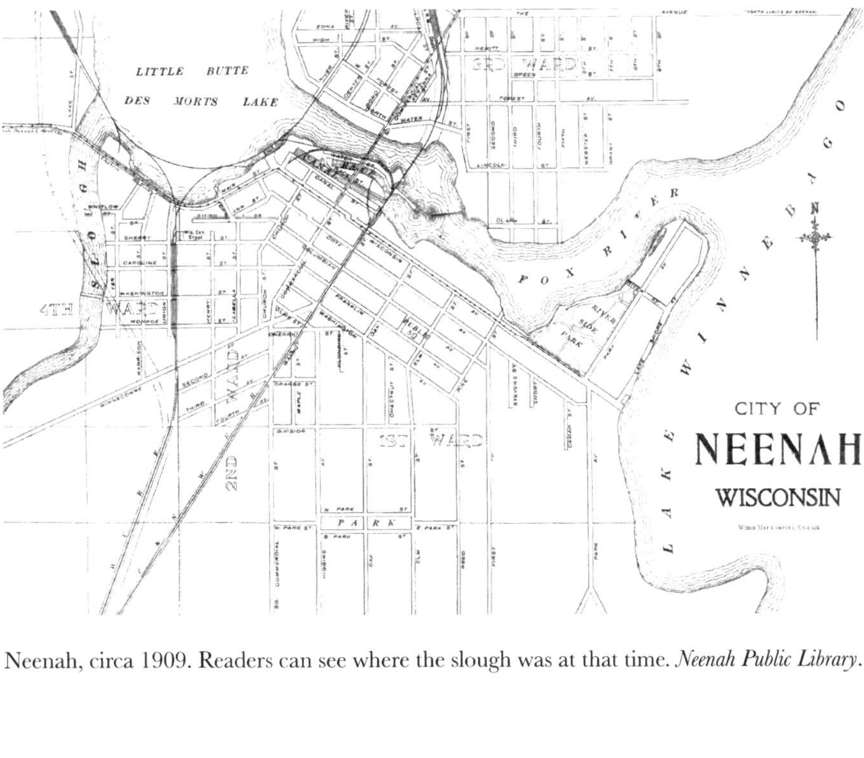

Neenah, circa 1909. Readers can see where the slough was at that time. *Neenah Public Library.*

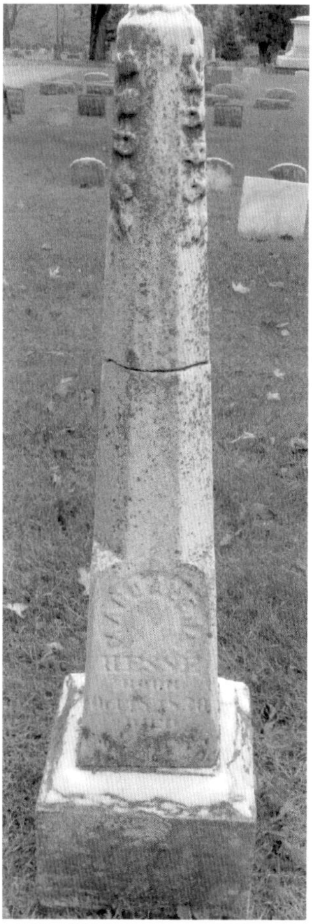

The grave of Magdalena Hesse; noticeably, her husband is not nearby. *Author's collection.*

well respected, his request was denied. Henry Wildfang, on behalf of the friends and family of Mrs. Hesse, expressed his heartfelt thanks to the community.

At the funeral, Sheriff Giddings arrested Julius Hesse, brother of John, as an accessory in the murder of Magdalena Hesse. District Attorney A.A. Austin charged that Julius had provided his brother with a weapon and a place to hide while carrying out his dastardly deed. Unable to pay the $1,000 bond, he was committed to the county jail.

Toward the end of March, attendance was up at the local temperance meeting, no doubt due to the Hesse case, which put alcoholism in the spotlight. A rousing discussion of politics also took place, with suggestions that local politicians (namely, the sheriff) did not take the effects of alcohol seriously and that voters should be aware of this.

The temperance movement had a long history in Neenah-Menasha, with newspaper accounts of meetings going back at least as far as 1855. Hardware store owner William Pitt Peckham was an early supporter, and the movement announced its goal in no uncertain terms: "The utter annihilation of the manufacture, sale and use of everything that can intoxicate man as a beverage." They sought to cure Neenah of the "red-eyed, blossom-nosed rummies."

The aforementioned C.B. Clark was added as an officer in 1870. Under his watch, the movement broadened its goal beyond the destruction of alcohol; it also hoped to encourage stimulating conversation. Many speakers were brought in that year, including a Union Pacific Railroad official and suffragette Elizabeth Cady Stanton (1815–1902), who spoke on a proposed "Sixteenth Amendment." (She wouldn't live to see the Nineteenth Amendment adopted in 1920, fifty years later.) Newspaperman Horace Greeley came in 1871. Clark, along with George Bergstrom and Charles Howard, took the profits from selling tickets and established Neenah's first public library.

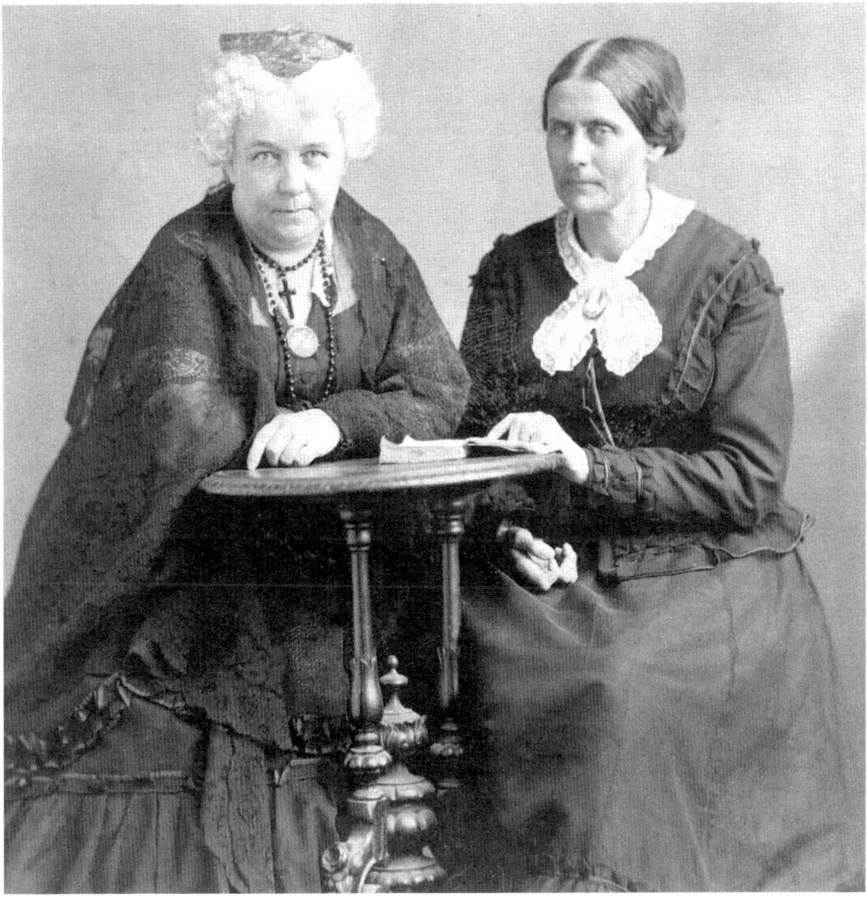

Elizabeth Cady Stanton (*left*) and Susan B. Anthony, the most famous of the nineteenth-century suffragists. *Author's collection.*

Hesse and the March 1871 temperance meeting were still on the minds of the people in April 1871, when local elections were held. It was a contest between the "Citizens Ticket" and the "Peoples Ticket," the former seen as the "law and order" crowd. Of course, those preaching law and order were victorious, with Judge Lyon and Constable Isaac L. Doton winning a majority.

The Hesse farm went up for sale in August 1871 and was said to contain one hundred acres of land at what is today the western end of Main Street. The property was situated one and a half miles west of the village limits. Of course, what was one mile west of the city in 1871 is now right back in the middle of Neenah.

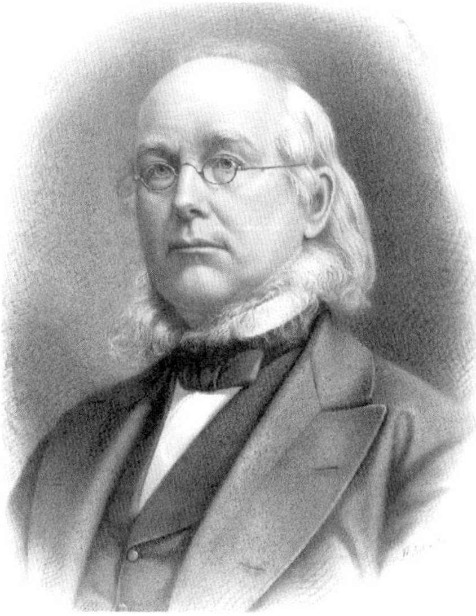

Right: Horace Greeley, legendary newspaperman and defender of the temperance movement. *Author's collection.*

Below: The first permanent library of Neenah, with books supplied by the Templars of the Crystal Lodge, a temperance society. *Neenah Historical Society.*

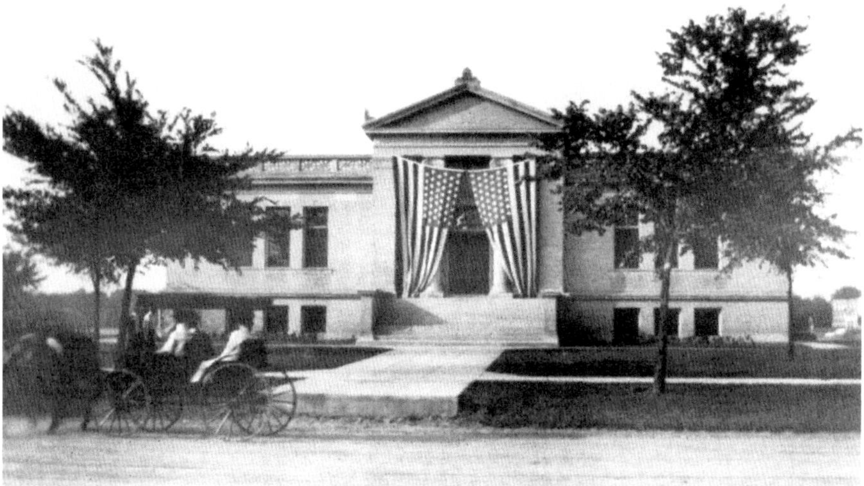

Theodore Brown of Neenah sent the older Hesse boys to an Ohio orphanage, while Caroline Friese Minck of Pennsylvania (Magdalena's sister) adopted her namesake niece Caroline, who went by Carrie.

Interestingly, the younger Caroline eventually reunited with her older brother Franklin. Franklin Hesse married a Neenah woman, Caroline Krull, in 1882. A year later, they became territorial pioneers in the Dakotas, specifically in the area of LaMoure, North Dakota. Descendants of their nine children can still be found there today. Carrie grew up in Philadelphia and married John Freyberger in Brooklyn, and they found their way to LaMoure in 1889. The Freybergers never had children, but John was very well known and respected for his grain exhibitions, most notably at the Panama-Pacific Exhibition of 1914. Representing his adopted state, Freyberger displayed a lighthouse constructed entirely of corn—an icon of pride hand-selected by Governor L.B. Hanna.

Since the time of the Hesse murder, the temperance movement grew both locally and nationally. On the local front, Neenah did become for a while a "dry" town, banning the sale of alcohol within city limits. Nationally, Rutherford B. Hayes was elected president of the United States in 1876; he was the first president to ever be a complete nondrinker. (It is believed that Donald Trump has never drank alcohol.) One White House observer of the day noted that at Hayes's parties, "The water flowed like champagne."

One last note of interest: Albert Huxley, one of the men on the coroner's jury who declared Magdalena's death a homicide, met a similar fate less than ten years later. His son-in-law Louis Emmonds shot Huxley in the head before turning the gun on himself.

2

HAMMER THE HAMMERER

Our next story bears some striking similarities to the first. For one thing, it takes place in Menasha, the sister city of Neenah, just on the other side of Doty Island. But the theme of alcohol abuse again crops up. Most of us can enjoy a drink and have a good time without incident. But the villain in this story, George Hammer, may have let the spirits get the better of him. Temperance did not take hold in Menasha quite as strongly as it did in Neenah, for a variety of complex reasons. But surely this story did not escape the attention of the church elders in Neenah.

We begin in the winter of 1878–79. Lars Oleson was an elderly, longtime resident of Menasha. Although he was known as a hard drinker and could become unruly when imbibing, the newspapers declared him "orderly and inoffensive" when sober. What happened behind closed doors is unknown, but the trouble was enough for his wife to have separated from him.

According to news reports, George Hammer was "a dissipated profligate young man, and a noted bruiser, famed for his strength." At the time of our story, Hammer would have been around twenty-eight years old, having grown up in Menasha's second ward while his father, Joseph, was a peddler.

On the evening of February 12, 1879, Oleson was at Harris's saloon in the Fourth Ward, enjoying pints of whiskey, when he ran into his good friend George Hammer.

Oleson invited Hammer and his wife, Minnie, to come to the Oleson residence for a round of drinks. A few rounds later, and somewhere in the interim, Oleson began pleading with Hammer and his wife to rent

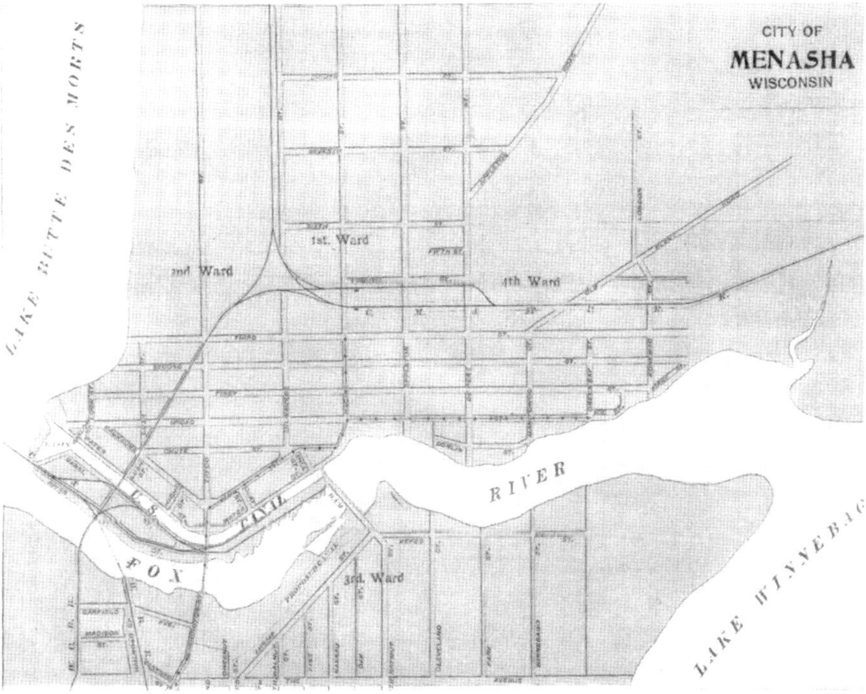

An early Menasha map that gives us a rough idea of where the Harris saloon was. *Menasha Historical Society.*

his house. Oleson was in need of money, but Hammer had no interest in the house. Oleson next allegedly tried to get Mrs. Hammer to spend the night with him (without George present), and this suggestion was not met with approval. Some insolent words were exchanged, and without warning a drunken Oleson rushed at George Hammer with an axe. Hammer deflected the blow with his arm, lacerating his hands in the process. In retaliation, he pummeled Oleson three or four times, which was all it took to knock the old man to the ground, blood gushing from his nose. Hammer propped his friend up on a pillow and gave him a glass of water, but Oleson would only babble incoherent nonsense.

At half past ten o'clock, Hammer made his way to Harris's saloon, washed up in the sink there and told the owner that he had severely injured his friend. The only other patron present was farmer Dennis R. Peebles, one of Menasha's few black men. Peebles was well respected in Menasha, having served in Company K of the First Regiment of the U.S. Colored Cavalry. His wife, Betsy, was a former slave who had worked for Governor Henry

Alexander Wise of Virginia. Hammer next stopped by Dr. Potter's residence and had him come back to look upon Oleson. A lifeless corpse lay on the ground, bruised but otherwise intact.

On Saturday, February 15, 1879, George Hammer was brought to Oshkosh and placed in the county jail. A coroner's inquest in front of Justice Silas Bullard followed. Doctors Potter and Fay—the same pair who had examined Magdalena Hesse—conducted the postmortem and found the cause of death to be exactly as Hammer claimed: several blows to the head. Specifically, one punch had crushed Oleson's nose beyond recognition and was more than likely the cause of his demise.

The inquest called Minnie Hammer, more popularly known as Minnie Diamond, on February 17, and she stunned those present with her beauty. The press reported that she was "quite pretty, with a delicate pale complexion and dark hair and eyes," wearing "a long and elegant cloak." She advised those present of the drinking, bickering and unexpected confrontation. Being the only witness besides the accused, her testimony carried great weight, and District Attorney George W. Burnell wrote out a formal complaint against her husband based on her story.

Further questioning of Diamond produced a minor scandal. She admitted that, although she was married to Hammer, she was not his lawful wife, as she had previously been married and never divorced. The district attorney was considering bigamy charges against her, but she tried to fend them off by suggesting she could disrupt the "best circles of society." Diamond claimed that, beyond her own faults, she knew a few things about the married men in town and would not be above embarrassing them to "raise a rumpus." Unfortunately for us, her claims were not recorded. The newspaper in Fond du Lac claimed that Diamond was well known in "police circles" as a certain Mrs. Smith but left the implication there.

Hammer's preliminary examination was set for February 21, and his initial story was very much the same as what Diamond had told at the coroner's inquest. The case appeared to be one of self-defense, only with the defender relying on excessive force in the process. Assisting Hammer with his defense were attorneys Elbridge Smith and Henry Fitzgibbon. You may recall Smith as John Hesse's unethical attorney. Fitzgibbon was born to Irish parents, and their influence on him was strong enough that many believed he had also been born there. He studied law at the office of James Clark Freeman in Oshkosh, followed by the law firm of Brown and Moses in Chicago before earning his degree in the latter city. From 1873 on, Fitzgibbon had his own practice in Menasha.

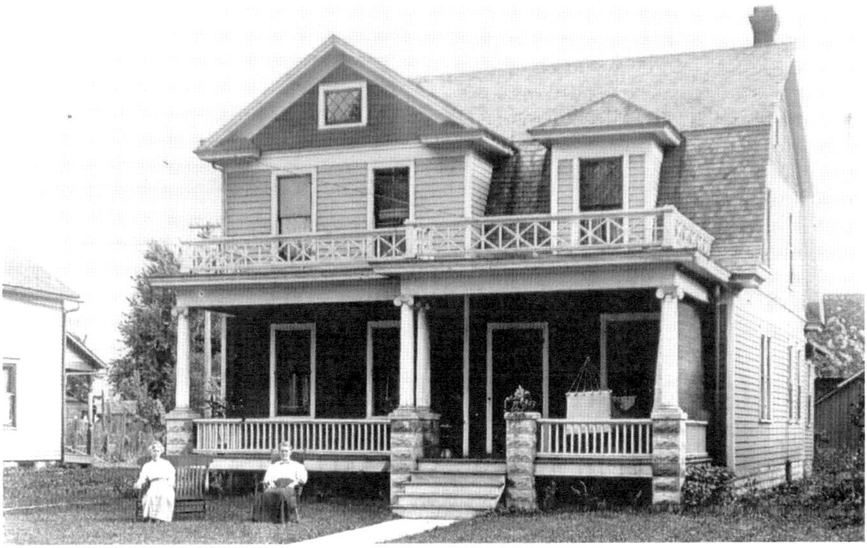

The Fitzgibbon home, as it was around the time of our story. *Menasha Historical Society*.

The trial began on April 22 with jury selection. The selection was not initially successful, with the pool not being enough to secure the necessary twelve men. The judge ordered the sheriff to lock the courthouse doors. Rather than call for more potential jurors, men were selected from the spectators in the courthouse that day. The process, although unorthodox, was quite successful, and the jury was sworn in by 5:30 in the evening.

Members of the selected jury were the following: John Thomas Harness, W.A. Neff, Franklin Howard, George Sawyer, farmer John Simpson, cabinetmaker Jacob Euler, S. Davis, Charles W. Bliss, William Abrams, farmer Henry Schroeder Sr., H.C. Ferguson and teacher Retire W. Frees (who shared this unusual name with an uncle). While it may seem obvious, it is also worth noting: there were no female jurors. In fact, no female jurors would exist for a great many years. Utah became the first state to include women in jury service, in 1898. Wisconsin did not allow women to serve on juries until 1921, and even then it was not universal. For example, in 1942, the Supreme Court case *Glasser v. United States* was needed to strike down legislation requiring women to take a jury class to serve as jurors. As late as 1968, women were still barred from serving in Mississippi.

The proceeding filled only one day in its entirety, April 23. Doctors Fay and Potter presented their postmortem analysis, highlighting the cause of death as a bruised nose and a concussion. Potter further commented how it was Hammer himself who had urged the doctor to attend to Oleson. Samuel S. Roby and Silas Bullard testified that they found the body when called to the house by the alarm. The prosecution's case relied entirely on those who saw Oleson after he was already dead; they had no firsthand accounts of the events inside his home during the alleged quarrel.

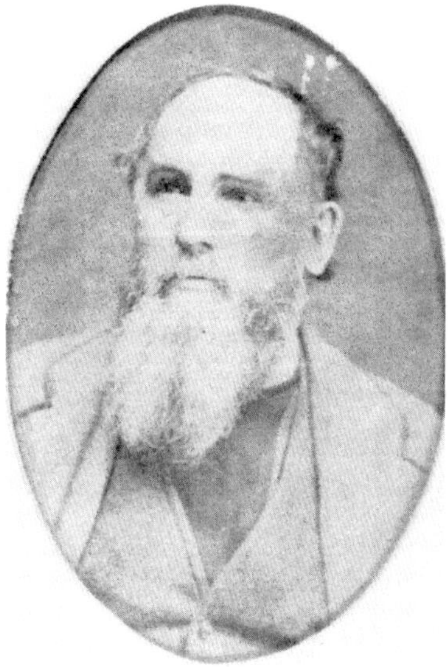

Samuel S. Roby was one of the first people to come across Lars Oleson following his death. *Menasha Historical Society.*

That same afternoon, attorney Smith presented the case for the defense. He began by agreeing to the facts as presented by the prosecution; his client did not deny killing Oleson but simply asserted that the motive was self-defense and not premeditation. Smith presented the relationship between Oleson and Hammer as one of great friendship and said the real trouble began because Oleson "was subject to fits of great passion" when drunk, a polite euphemism for Oleson's attempt to improperly seduce Mrs. Hammer. Smith argued that Hammer's propping his injured friend on a pillow and fetching Dr. Potter were clear signs that he did not try to conceal what happened, an altercation that quickly grew out of hand.

Smith's primary defense witnesses were George Hammer and his wife, who (not surprisingly) told essentially the same story as each other and Smith. With no one else present to contradict them, their version of events was the only one available to the jury. The verdict would ultimately come down to how trustworthy the Hammer couple appeared.

On April 24, the jury found Hammer guilty only of manslaughter in the fourth degree. Having convinced the jury that he was acting in self-defense, George Hammer could face only a fine or a maximum of two years in prison.

At sentencing, Hammer's only words were that his testimony was honest and that he stood by his claims. Judge David Judson Pulling expressed his reservations about the verdict, saying that he was not happy that the only witnesses were hardly impartial. He felt, at the very least, that Hammer should have called in someone to vouch for his good character, but no such witness

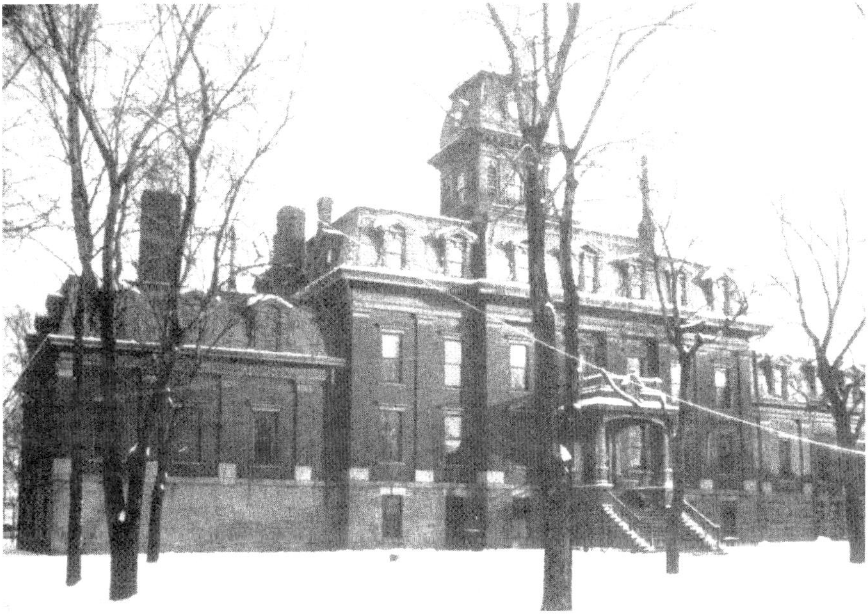

The Winnebago County Courthouse around 1885, already slightly expanded. *Neenah Historical Society.*

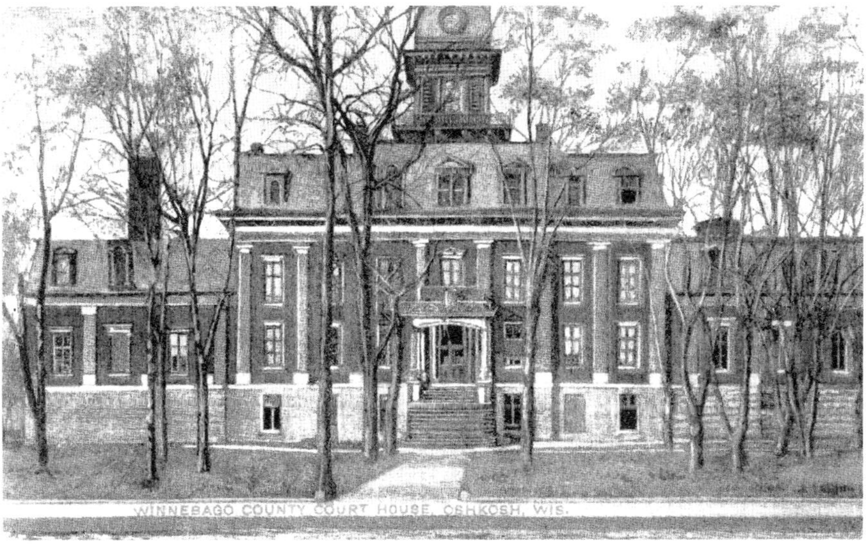

The earliest known image of the Winnebago County Courthouse, possibly as John Hesse would have seen it. *Keith Vincent.*

was found. Pulling instead informed Hammer that he had been known as a "frequenter of saloons and low places and the companion of common prostitutes." Pulling said he had known Hammer as a boy and found him to be a good child with above average intelligence who, nonetheless, strayed from the right path. If he had just applied himself better, he could have been an upstanding member of society. Feeling there was hope for him yet, Pulling handed down the sentence of one year in prison, with three days of that sentence to be spent in solitary confinement. All in all, it was a very modest punishment for what may have been a passionate murder.

Within days of Hammer's sentencing, Minnie Diamond was picked up by police in Oshkosh for vagrancy. While intoxicated, she said she had "cut loose" from Hammer and would not lie on his behalf anymore. She further suggested that she had been forced to raise money in indecent ways to pay for his legal defense. The following morning, Justice Jackson decided against any criminal punishment and instead ordered her to leave the city by the four o'clock train. Were Diamond's words merely the ramblings of a drunken woman, or had there been a cover-up? Was the Oleson murder really self-defense?

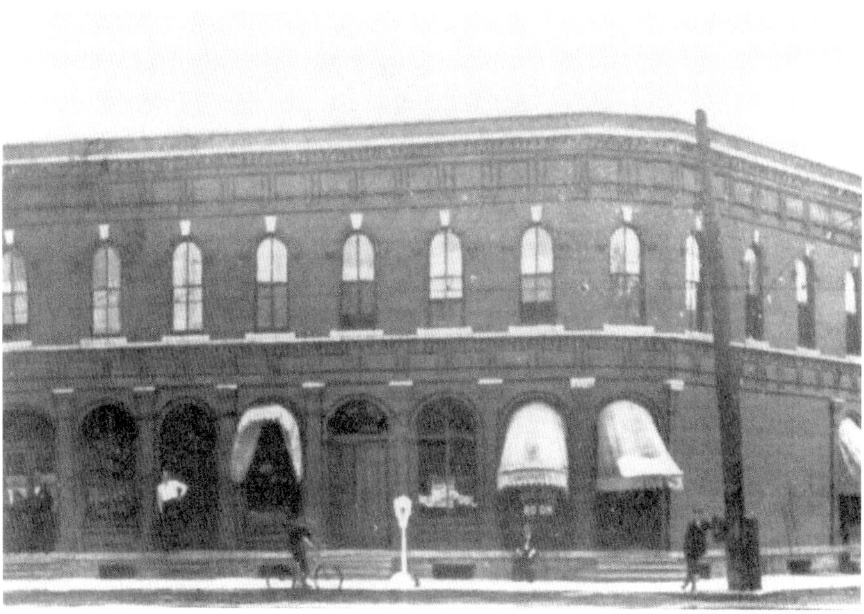

The Landgraf Hotel, at one time the pride of Menasha. *Menasha Historical Society.*

On his release from Waupun, it did not take long for George Hammer to again come to the attention of the Menasha police. In February 1881, he was arrested for "assault to commit great bodily harm" to one Peter Nelson, a Danish farmer. Judge Max M. Schoetz ordered Hammer back to jail. At trial in April, Nelson said that Hammer had literally chased him down, tackled him and "pounded" him while threatening murder until police arrived to pull the convict off of him. Hammer pled guilty to a lesser charge of simple assault and was returned to the jail.

Schoetz went on to some local distinction, perhaps with a little help from his father-in-law, Andrew Landgraf (proprietor of the city's biggest hotel). Around 1882, he formed a partnership with the aforementioned Elbridge Smith, which continued until Smith died in 1894; then Schoetz entered into a partnership with Silas Bullard. Schoetz became city attorney of Menasha and, in 1894, was the Democratic nominee for member of the assembly. His Republican opponent was Silas Bullard, his own law partner. Bullard won the friendly contest. Schoetz organized the Menasha Building and Loan Association and was one of the organizers and a stockholder in the First National Bank of Menasha. To top it all off, he served two terms as the city's mayor.

In contrast to Schoetz, the futures for Hammer and Diamond were apparently not very bright. Though I have made every effort, both of these vile creatures seem to have simply vanished from the face of the earth. No news reports, census records or other trace of them has been found. Your curiosity as to their final years will have to remain unsated.

3

THE CHINESE RIOTS

Although their numbers were never large, it may come as a surprise to many that America, even small-town Wisconsin, had Chinese neighborhoods as far back as the 1850s. Chinese immigrants were in Wisconsin before the Jewish wave of immigrants and before the Italians. For obvious racial reasons, they did not assimilate as easily, but despite these prejudices, several Chinese men were able to operate thriving businesses and support their families. The vast majority of these businesses were "Chinese laundries," and that was no different in Kaukauna.

News accounts show Chinese in Fond du Lac in 1874 and in Portage in 1879, and the earliest recorded Kaukauna laundry dates to 1885, the same year as the city's incorporation. By that time, a racial myth had already become attached to the Chinese. Because the majority of Chinese immigrants were bachelors, rumors were spread that young, white boys and girls were lured into Chinese opium dens and forced to be sex slaves by their "oriental" masters. The rumors were exacerbated by the Chinese Exclusion Act of 1882; even if the businessmen were successful, they couldn't legally bring over their wives or daughters, guaranteeing an almost exclusively male population. Today, we know the "opium fiend" is a caricature built on falsehoods, but it was a mainstream view in that age.

We do not know exactly when the first Chinese immigrant came to Kaukauna. By July 1885, Wing Lee was advertising in the local newspaper, and it was reported that his business was located on "Finnegan's Block" at the busy intersection of Crooks and Second and was doing quite well.

Whether the laundry had just opened or had been there for years is not known. We do know that it was successful enough to remain open for many years after.

The old rumors started up again in Milwaukee, with claims that Chinese laundry workers were luring girls fourteen and younger into their shops for "immoral purposes." The Milwaukee and Madison newspapers ran stories on March 6, 1889, speculating that "Chinese demons" had "enticed" as many as twenty-two white girls into their "dens" in Milwaukee for the purpose of being sold off as brides in Chicago. The kernel of truth here is that some white women did apparently visit Chinese laundries for romantic reasons. But they may not have been forced—one woman testified to having visited a laundryman no fewer than twelve times in three months, each time of her own volition. There is another shocking fact to consider: prior to the 1920s, the age of marital consent in Wisconsin (and in much of the Midwest) was ten. Some of the "women" involved may well have been children by modern standards.

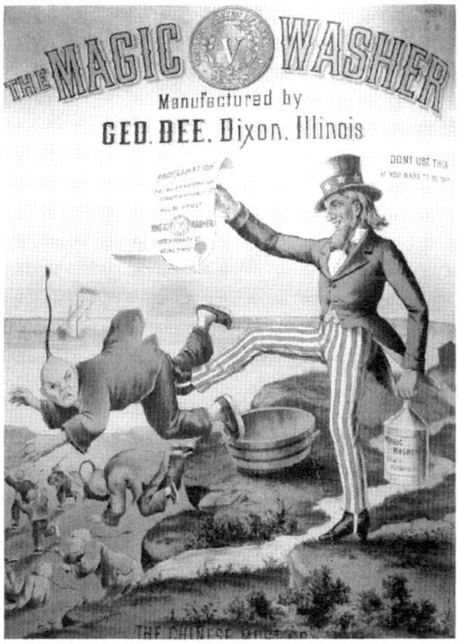

A poster showing how America (Uncle Sam) felt about the Chinese in the late 1800s. *Author's collection.*

Regardless of the truth, the race mixing was a shock, and a riot broke out on March 11 that lasted four days and was said to have involved three thousand Milwaukee men and the destruction of a dozen Chinese businesses. As many as one thousand men at a time would circle a laundry while pelting the windows with bricks. The men marched through the streets, chanting, "Get a rope!" and with cries to "string them up to a lamppost." This had a lasting effect, dropping the number of Chinese laundries in Milwaukee from twenty-eight to thirteen by the end of the year. The number never went above twelve throughout the 1890s.

As an outgrowth of the Milwaukee riots, a smaller melee ensued in Kaukauna on March 15, 1889. Earlier in the day, six Chinese men arrived in Kaukauna from Milwaukee, having been chased out of the latter city. They took up temporary residence at the laundry, but that same day, the Kaukauna riot broke out. The front of the building was smashed in, causing those inside to literally run for their lives. A mob of boys and men busted into Wing Lee's south-side laundry, yelling, "The Chinese must go!" Wing was not aware of any problem until a large stone came through his window, breaking his lamp and hitting a stove. A fire broke out, and Wing could barely contain the blaze with a blanket and a pail of water. One Chinese American was beaten in the stomach with a brick. The *Kaukauna Times*, to its credit, called the mob "entirely uncalled for" and a "shameful proceeding," resting the blame on law enforcement's unwillingness to intervene.

Upon fleeing Kaukauna, Wing Lee took a train to Appleton and then to Oshkosh, where he took up residence with Hop Chung, who had a tea store at 10 High Street. Hop telegraphed to Chicago, requesting the assistance of Wong Jim Foo. Wing was justifiably upset, telling the newspapers that "he has always dealt honestly with Kaukauna people and behaved himself like a man." In June, Wing Lee, proprietor of the south-side laundry, filed a claim of damage against the city for $550.

On August 16, 1889, it was reported that the Chinese riot case with the City of Kaukauna had been settled with a payment of $250. This, however, does not seem to be true, according to an article that appeared in the *Oshkosh Northwestern* around the same time. Hop Chung threatened to sue the city for damages he sustained there the previous spring.

> *One of the newspapers said that the city of Kaukauna had paid me the loss I sustained there last winter. I wish the public to know that I have received nothing from the city of Kaukauna. I paid Charles Foy $500 for the laundry and business and afterwards expended $40 in repairing it. My brother lost in cash $156 and May Long $60. When my laundry was broken into and the washing lost and destroyed, that I paid for. It amounted to more than $50. There are not only business and personal losses there are also legal expenses in obtaining consul to come here from Chicago. The city of Kaukauna can settle with me if it pays me enough to cover my losses.*

At a common council meeting in October 1889, a letter was received from Oshkosh. It was from the Chinese American whose property had been destroyed in the riot on the south side of Kaukauna. It stated that the case could be settled by the payment of $550 and all costs incurred. The *Kaukauna Times* wrote in an editorial that this case should be settled at once, noting that the sooner it was settled the less the cost to settle. There was no doubt the city was responsible for the property that was destroyed, as no police officers even attempted to stop the rioting. Let the city settle and then have those who participated in the riot arrested and punished. The

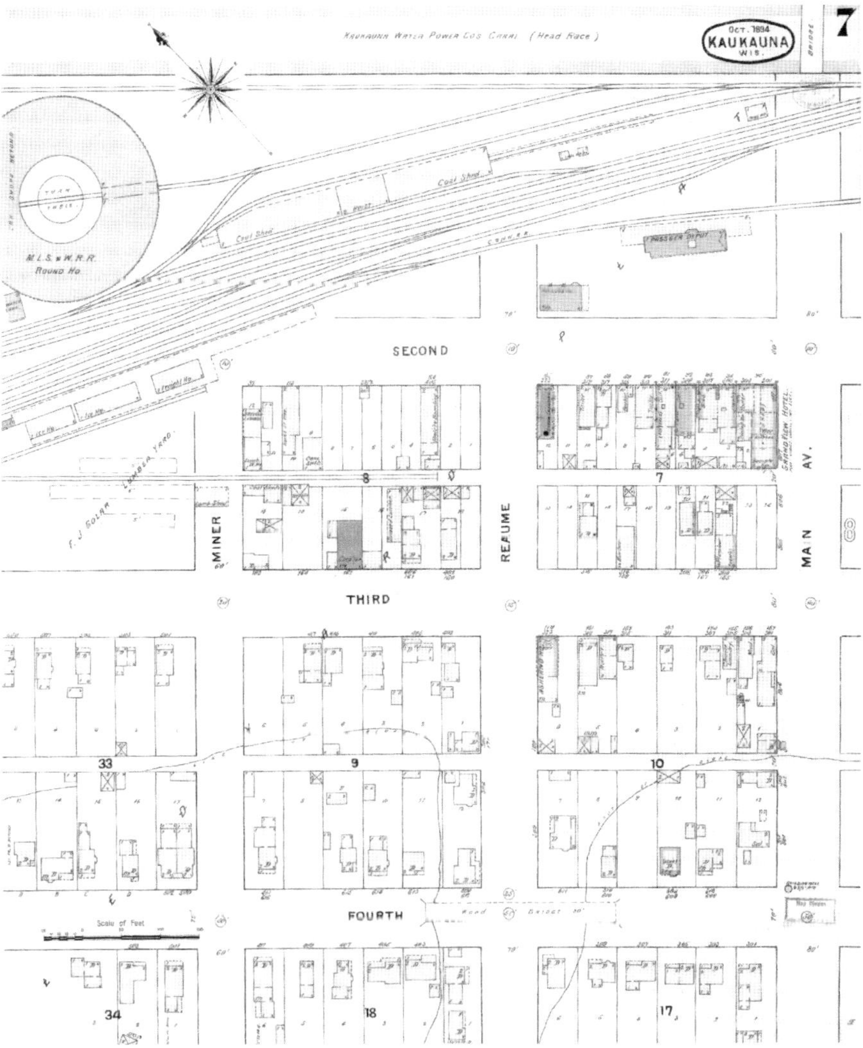

A fire map of Kaukauna in 1894, showing the location of a new steam laundry. *Kaukauna Public Library*.

paper specifically criticized William Sludy, the marshal of the south side. Despite his important position, Sludy is today something of an enigma, appearing in no known records. All we know of him is what appears in a short newspaper article in 1892, where—along with William Snyder and Thomas Solar—he was found to be assisting a brothel through the use of physical battery on troublemakers. Not exactly the sort of behavior we expect from a man of the law.

Although a prominent businessman in Oshkosh, Hop Chung's life there was not without its problems. In July 1890, William Nintzel was accused of giving Chung a "drubbing" and using his umbrella to smash the tearoom's front window. That same month, unease was still present in Kaukauna. Moy Len had taken over the Kaukauna laundry, and one James Kelly demanded some work be done immediately. Moy Len explained that he would have to wait for other orders to be completed, and the irate Kelly punched the laundryman "belly hald" (very hard), according to the *Kaukauna Times*. Kelly was given thirty days in the local jail. Moy Len was reported to have said, "Bon he le long ge hue, Melican man no monkee Chinee." (I am unable to decipher this broken English; perhaps something about "American man can't make a monkey out of the Chinese"?) By the summer of 1891, even Hop Chung, said to be the head of Oshkosh's "Chinese colony," had had enough and moved to Chicago.

Around 1897, Moy Len died and was unceremoniously buried in the Kelso Cemetery, just north of the city limits. With his passing, the city's willingness to accept Chinese laundries seemed quite strained. An anonymous advertisement in the *Kaukauna Times* was printed on May 14, 1897: "The Chinese laundry which you started up on Second Street a couple months ago was closed up yesterday and the fixtures removed. The Kaukauna steam laundry covers the field here thoroughly; no almond eyes heathen of the Middle Kingdom need apply." The sentiment speaks for itself.

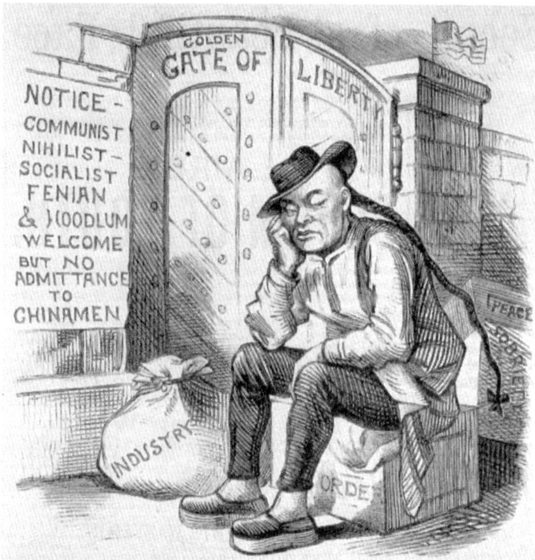

THE ONLY ONE BARRED OUT.
Enlightened American Statesman.—"We must draw the line *somewhere*, you know."

A political cartoon showing immigration and the door closed to the Chinese. *Author's collection.*

Moy Len's memory was not soon forgotten. The *Kaukauna Times* saw fit to report in April 1901 how a countryman from Oshkosh came to Kaukauna to visit the grave. The old stereotypes returned, with the visitor referred to as a "Celestial" and a "disciple of Confucius" without ever mentioning his name. The visitor left on the grave a roasted pork loin, a roasted chicken, six hard-boiled eggs, six red apples and four glasses of whiskey. Incense was burned, and a "row of fancy colored sky rockets" was set off. This kind gesture was witnessed by many curious onlookers, all of whom were respectful.

The Chinese laundry business made its last hiccup in Kaukauna around September 1911, when Willie Moy of Appleton opened his business in the Canham building on the south side, next to the post office. In February, he moved this business to the north side on Wisconsin Avenue, in a storefront formerly occupied by a Mrs. Johnson and her millinery store. By all indications, this second location did not last much longer than the first, and Willie Moy may have been the last Chinese merchant in Kaukauna for several decades.

The legacy of the Milwaukee riot (and its Kaukauna and Oshkosh offshoots) is small, as the event has been largely forgotten, overshadowed by the so-called Bayview Massacre of 1886. But, according to historian Victor Jew, the Milwaukee event was the only midwestern anti-Chinese riot in history and for that reason deserves to be remembered. Today, Chinese Americans are most often associated with San Francisco, but this accident of history could have gone another way.

4

THE STRANGE AND SORDID TALE OF PORTER ROSS

In Wisconsin's history, there have been many unusual criminal happenings. Our cannibalistic killers—Ed Gein and Jeffrey Dahmer—are legendary. Our northwoods was a vacationing spot for Al Capone. But one of the strangest cases of all revolves around a resident of Kaukauna—Porter Ross—who made a mockery of the justice system in one of Outagamie County's most degrading cases. The *Kaukauna Times* called the event "one of the most blood curdling that has ever been recorded in this county."

On March 14, 1851, Governor Nelson Dewey signed an act to appoint a three-member prison commission to select a site for the state penitentiary. Waupun was chosen on July 4, 1851, for two primary reasons: it was near the proposed Rock River Valley Railroad (RRV), and the locale was surrounded by quality limestone for construction. A temporary prison was started that same month. The original permanent building was constructed in 1854. It contained 288 cells and was built using convict labor, coming to a total cost of roughly $325 per cell, or $93,600 overall. The RRV, incidentally, extended from Fond du Lac to the newly created village of Minnesota Junction (near Waupun) in 1854. Although it was named "Minnesota Junction" with the intention of having the railroad continue westward, the line was never built.

The main administration building was erected in 1855; the large, ornate, stone-and-iron wall was added in 1858. An interesting side note is that Waupun housed all of the state's inmates—male and female—until the women were transferred to Taycheedah in 1933.

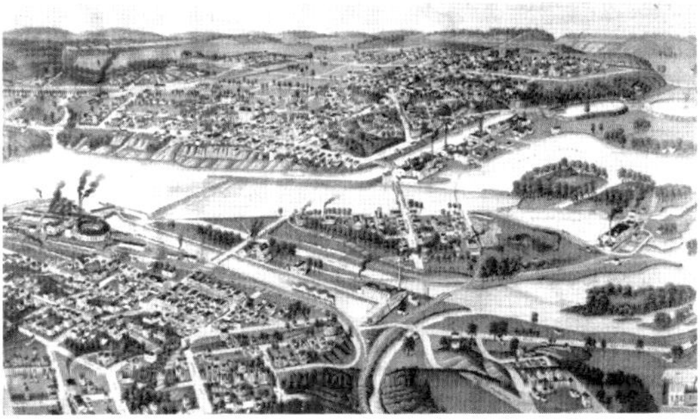

Left: An overview of Kaukauna, as seen around 1886. *Kaukauna Public Library*.

Below: Waupun Prison in one of its earlier incarnations, as Porter Ross would have seen it. *Author's collection*.

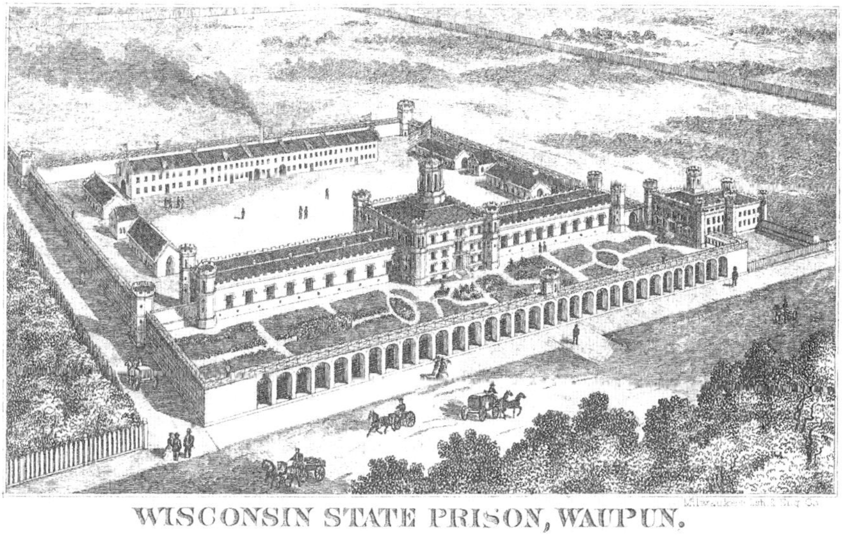

Porter Ross was born in Erie County, New York, in 1842. His parents, both New York natives, were Daniel and Polly Ross. In 1860, Porter was sent to Waupun Prison from Walworth County for unknown reasons at age seventeen. His stay was less than two years. With Waupun's buildings less than ten years old, young Porter was living in a state-of-the-art prison.

When the Union needed young men to serve during the Civil War, Porter grudgingly obliged. He enrolled in Shawano as a private in the Sixteenth Wisconsin Infantry, Company D, on January 2, 1862. He was anything but a model soldier, though, becoming a degenerate "bounty jumper" and deserting his crew as early as May 6, 1862. He was possibly scared off when all of the members of the six-man color guard were killed on April 6, 1862, in the Battle of Shiloh. This was the first and only battle Ross took part in; he missed out on the remainder of his comrades' struggles at Vicksburg and as part of Sherman's March to the Sea. Who knows what could have become of Porter Ross? Rather than a scoundrel, he might instead have been remembered as a war hero. But it was not to be.

In 1867, while employed as a farmer, Porter was sent back to Waupun Prison from Rock County for unknown reasons. He was given the number 1264 and was finally released again on August 12, 1870, with time served.

Ross found himself a wife, Diana Palmer Sears, shortly after leaving prison the second time. Diana was born in New York in 1845 to John Sears and Patty Foarel Sears. They were married in Shawano on December 23, 1872. Some sources suggest December 25, 1873, though this would be within one month of their eldest daughter's birth (certainly possible, of course, even if socially frowned upon). There followed three children: Mary in January 1874, Charlotte in 1876 and John in 1879.

The Ross family was living on farmland in Spring Water, Waushara County, in 1880. Daughter Mary died there on April 29, 1882, at age eight and was buried in Saxeville. Charlotte died later that same year, at six years of age. More children were to come. Katie Ross was born in 1883 while the family lived in Richmond, near Shawano. After moving to Kaukauna in 1886, they were blessed with another daughter, Carrie, in 1888. Upon moving to Kaukauna, Ross took up work as a mason. Then, tragedy struck when Diana died in Kaukauna on April 24, 1891, aged forty-five.

Shortly after Mrs. Ross's death, Porter was told of a young woman in DePere named Nellie Duprey. His neighbor had recommended her to him as a "first-class housekeeper." Porter met Nellie at the home of her father in DePere and took her on as a housekeeper along with her two children from a prior relationship, Mamie and Willie. Porter knew she was a woman with questionable morals, but she swore her faithfulness to him, and he accepted her oath as sincere.

The pair were married on July 12, 1892, in Kaukauna by the justice of the peace, Michael H. Mulloy. Their witnesses were Christ V. Burch and Charles Pope. Burch had been a prominent Kaukauna south-sider going back decades. Pope was possibly a resident of Neenah. If that wily stonecutter Porter Ross had known the family history of Nellie Duprey when he married her, he might have had second thoughts. While his reputation was not spectacular, and hers was no better, her family's was even more unusual.

The Duprey clan had lived in the Green Bay area for a great many years, settling in DePere. Jean Baptiste Duprey came to the area in the early 1800s, when Wisconsin was still part of Michigan Territory and populated exclusively by U.S. troops. Jean Baptiste, a Frenchman, had been trained and educated to become a Roman Catholic priest but turned away from his calling to marry a Chippewa Indian woman.

Jean Baptiste's marriage was evidently not a happy one. He and his wife were living in DePere in 1855 when the woman, now blind, attempted to kill her husband in his sleep. Her blindness was so severe, though, that in an attempt to grab his throat she had actually taken hold of his leg and nearly cut off his foot with a knife. This marriage produced three sons, one being Thomas Duprey, the father of Nellie Ross and her sister Katie Duprey.

In 1893, Ross was living "on the north side of 13th, two houses north of Main." The exact address is unclear; in Kaukauna, a house cannot be north or south of Main. One evening in the first week of October 1893, there was a noise coming from the cellar of the Charles H. Hodges residence in Kaukauna. Hodges, a locomotive engineer, was living on Reaume Avenue at the northwest corner of Fourth. Mrs. Hodges heard the noise but, with her husband away, did not care to investigate. The following morning, the cellar was checked, and it was determined that roughly twenty cans of fruit and a jar of butter had been removed.

Marshal Julius Kuehn was notified and arrived on the scene to search for clues. Kuehn, a man of many talents, was very respected in town. More than anything else, he was known as a successful businessman, having leased properties to others for their businesses, such as T.H. Warren's dry-goods store on Second Street. He had invested in all sorts of new projects, including an elevator in 1885, also on Second Street. Kuehn's blacksmith shop, on the northwest corner of Crooks Avenue and Second Street, is today a historic landmark.

Julius was experienced in the field of danger, having walked away from an explosion on February 21, 1887. He was in his shop, pounding on a hot piece of iron with his hammer, when a spark flew into a nearby cigar box. As chance would have it, Julius stored his gunpowder in this box and thought little of it until this point. The resulting explosion took out seventeen panes of glass and sent Julius (along with hammer and tongs) several feet back from his anvil. No one else was in the room, and Julius walked away unscathed.

Kuehn found the ground near the Hodges home to be soft, and there were easily identifiable footprints near the cellar door—those of a man's foot and those of a boy who appeared to have accompanied him. Kuehn, having "sized up" the residents of that part of town, decided to search the domicile of Porter Ross. Kuehn ascertained that the prints were comparable to shoes owned by Ross.

Kuehn called in to the residence, but there was no answer, as Ross was absent. Julius began a thorough search and did indeed find the fruit stored away in Ross's cellar. The butter, however, appeared to be missing. Hodges identified the missing fruit, and Kuehn waited at the Ross residence for Porter's return, at which time he was placed under arrest.

But Ross was not ready to go willingly and took off running. Kuehn pursued Ross and was able to successfully knock him to the floor. Ross struggled, but after having his head slammed repeatedly into the floor, Ross gave up every last ounce of fight in him. Ross was later arraigned before Squire Michael H. Mulloy (the same man who had officiated his wedding) and was given the choice of a fine of twenty-five dollars or three months in jail. Ross paid up.

Things didn't stay quiet for long. Nellie had Porter arrested in Kaukauna in 1894, claiming that he had tried to shoot her but missed. The case went as far as the city court, where the matter was quickly dropped.

After the shooting incident, the couple moved to Aniwa for six weeks and then moved again to Shawano, where they were counted for the 1895 census. Memorial Day 1896 proved to be a turning point for the couple when, after three years of marriage, Nellie again began her old lifestyle at the urgings of her sister Katherine. Despite these disturbances, Shawano was a place Porter found acceptable enough, and he was able to live there until December 1896. At that point, he moved on to Menominee.

Throughout the years, Nellie repeatedly left Porter for other men, but he was always able to persuade her to come home and give up her "life of shame." However, Menominee was the couple's downfall. While walking the streets on December 29, Porter discovered that Nellie and her sister—using the alias "Katie LaClair"—were keeping rented rooms in town. Porter again persuaded Nellie to come home, but she fled to Winneconne on New Year's Day.

Nellie returned home the next day with her sister but left again a few hours later when Katie told the police that Porter had physically assaulted her. Katie also claimed that just prior to the "pounding," he sent her a letter in which he threatened to kill her. The following morning, he had a jury trial and was again acquitted.

Porter left Menominee in the middle of February 1897 and again took up residence in Kaukauna "on the island" and found work as a stonemason. His wife and her sister did not join him, instead taking up residence in a godforsaken place north of Menominee known as "the shanties." After this, they again returned home to their father's house in DePere but were also occasionally seen on the streets of Kaukauna.

Nellie and Katie visited the "resorts" near Kaukauna and also the ones in Appleton. Porter had found Nellie taking up residence in an Appleton resort on Saturday, February 27. If the implication remains unclear to the reader, "resort" was a newspaper euphemism for brothel. He tried to convince Nellie to return home with him but was unable to do so this time. Porter was scared away from the residence when the "woman of the house" appeared from upstairs with a revolver under her apron, and that was the last he saw of Nellie for over a week.

Porter was at home between two and three o'clock in the afternoon on Monday, March 8, when his attention was directed by his daughter to a horse-drawn carriage. Watching the sleigh and team of horses go by, he saw that the vehicle contained his wife, her sister Katie and two men unknown to him. With his new residence and job firmly in place, the last thing he wanted was any distractions. When his wife waved at him in a mocking manner, though, he became enraged and quickly took his pistol from a shelf and put the weapon into his pocket. His maid, Miss Bertha Mills (sometimes identified as "Gertie Mills"), witnessed him grabbing for the pistol, a .38-caliber American Bull Dog revolver that held five rounds. It had been in Porter's possession for some time and was, admittedly, an old gun.

Porter went directly to the livery stable and hired a horse and cutter. He followed the carriage just northeast of the city limits in the direction of a boardinghouse owned and operated by Louise Brockman Beaulieu. The house, typical for the two sisters, was of a very poor reputation. Its precise location lay one and a half miles east of Kaukauna toward Wrightstown, along the river road with the racetrack adjoined to the resort. On the way, he passed Charles McCarthy walking to town, and they may have exchanged pleasantries.

Upon reaching the house, he spotted the party's team of horses hitched in front of the building as he had expected. He, too, hitched up his horses and went inside.

Porter was greeted by a young man (later found to be Fred Schabo of Appleton) sitting in the left-hand corner of the front room and also by Mrs. Beaulieu. She had been forewarned of his possible coming by one of the women, probably Katie. Porter inquired about the two women, and Louise informed him that they were upstairs. When he asked about the other man (who was later found to be Phillip Brown of Appleton), she confirmed that he was upstairs with the women. Porter asked Schabo if he was the driver of the rig that brought the four out to the boardinghouse. He denied the accusation, stating, "I am a stranger here. I just came from Canada."

Porter instructed Beaulieu's young maid, Amelia Yetke, to watch his horse, and he went upstairs with the resort's owner. Ross had told her he had a warrant for the women's arrest, and she assisted him on that pretense. She instructed the three to open the door, and they would not. When she demanded again, they unlocked and opened the door. The two women were in the middle of the room, and Phillip was standing to the left of the door with his coat off. Porter approached his wife, placed his hand on her shoulder and said, "My God, Nellie. I have caught you in another place, same as I did a week ago [in Appleton]." When he urged her to come home with him, she retorted, "Go away! I will not live with you or have anything to do with you. I am going to lead a gay life and a fast one." Porter became quite perturbed and threatened her with a warrant for her arrest.

While the four (without Brown) walked back downstairs, Nellie turned to her sister and said, "My God, Katie! You have led me to this." After Beaulieu had returned to the front room, the three family members congregated in the kitchen with Schabo and began talking with each other. Unfortunately, any chance for a peaceful resolution was long gone. Porter took hold of Fred's coat and asked him to go outside for a moment. Schabo refused the offer, but Porter insisted again. Katie suddenly said to Schabo, "Fred, kill the old son of a bitch." Fred reacted and pushed Porter into a table that was against the wall.

Porter was hit across the face between his cheek and nose and was pushed hard enough that his elbow flew back through a window. Nellie started to egg Schabo on, yelling, "Give it to him, Fred! Give it to him!" Porter, thinking he "was getting the worst of it," pulled out his revolver and shot at Schabo. Schabo fell back, holding his chest. Seeing he had been shot, Schabo took off for the road.

Porter next shot at Katie, who had tripped over Nellie while trying to run back upstairs. She was shot in the right breast above her lung. The bullet hit in just such a way that, upon entering her chest, it fell into the cavity of her lung, where it could not be removed.

Nellie was hit by a bullet intended for Schabo and, at this point, informed Porter, "I will go home and live with you, but I am shot." One of the stray bullets had grazed her right shoulder, making a "skin wound." When she turned to walk away, Porter stood in the doorway between the kitchen and front room and shot Nellie in the back. She fell down face-first, bludgeoning her face on the door casing at the foot of the stairs. This bullet was far more direct. In an unlikely fashion, it entered her back under the right shoulder blade and somehow managed to exit at the base of her forehead between her eyes, if newspaper accounts are to be believed.

Katie staggered into the front room, informing Beaulieu that she was shot. Fred Schabo had since returned and was stumbling out a back door when Louise called him back in to go fetch a doctor. He told her that he wasn't able to get far, as he was shot, too. Fred was luckier than both women, as his wound was simply a flesh wound and not life-threatening. He was shot on the left side under the lower rib, and the bullet had lodged in his right hip bone. His abdomen muscles were slightly torn, but his internal organs remained unharmed. When he was treated later that day by Dr. Charles D. Boyd, the bullet was easily extracted. Brown was back in the front room by now. As it turned out, he had broken the upstairs window and jumped out, but he returned when he was called back by Fred, who had been outside momentarily before he realized he had forgotten his hat.

When the macabre event was over and Porter saw what he had done, he said to himself, "My God, what have I done? I have killed my poor wife." Brown watched as Ross turned the gun on himself and fired, but all the chambers were empty. The fifth and final bullet was lodged in the wall near the stairway, another one that had missed Schabo. Porter instead left the residence, spotting two previously unnoticed men (neither Brown nor Schabo) running away in the direction of Wrightstown.

On the ride back home, Porter came across Charles McCarthy again, still heading into town. Charles was just about to reach the railroad tracks where they cross Lawe Street, roughly the intersection with Delanglade Street. Said Porter to McCarthy, "I have killed three of them since I saw you last."

He repeated this assertion of three deaths when he reached the depot, where Chief of Police Daniel Reardon was. "I went out there with the intention of killing them all and myself." Reardon asked for the revolver, but Porter replied that he was perfectly capable of hanging on to it himself. The officer, somewhat surprised by the straight-faced response, was able to eventually get the gun from him. Porter was placed into the local lockup for a few hours before District Attorney John Bottensek arrived on the 6:25 p.m. train. Both men (Porter and Bottensek) were already headed back to Appleton by the 7:01 p.m. train. Chief Reardon's origins are somewhat interesting. Unlike many men of the Fox Cities who had served in the Union army during the Civil War, Reardon spent his infancy in war-torn South Carolina. While obviously not engaged in battle himself, it is entirely possible that many of his family had fired at (or been shot by) the brave men of Kaukauna.

Shortly after the affray, Dr. Charles Boyd and Dr. Osborn G. Lord were summoned to care for the three wounded at the boardinghouse. (Early reports had stated that the doctors present were Boyd and David A. Titus, but this seems to have been incorrect.) Somehow, in an unexplained manner, Louise Beaulieu had received a minor "scalp wound" and needed a bandage for the damage done. Boyd is a notable Kaukauna figure, serving as mayor in 1901; he went on to greater acclaim for founding the Riverview Sanatorium (tuberculosis clinic) in 1914. Dr. Lord's mark on Kaukauna is felt today in Veterans Memorial Park; the physician donated the centerpiece statue honoring all Civil War veterans.

After the murder was discovered, a coroner's jury was hastily assembled. The jury members were the following: liveryman Thomas Malone of 332 Wisconsin Avenue, police officer Richard Conlon, paper manufacturer Christ W. Larson, Nicholas M. Kettenhofen, waterworks engineer William H. Hyland and Peter Lappens.

The jury members examined the body of Nellie Ross and also the premises where she was killed. They then adjourned until nine o'clock the next morning.

That same Monday evening, Porter was taken before Judge Mitchell—who now had the revolver in his possession—for examination. Acting as Porter's attorney was Alfred A. Nugent, a seasoned veteran in multiple senses of the term.

Nugent had served his second country—he was born in Canada—during the Civil War. At the unthinkably tender age of fifteen, young Alfred enlisted as a private in the Twenty-First Wisconsin Infantry, Company I, in December 1863. He was with his regiment on the top of Lookout Mountain in the winter of 1863–64 and later was with General William Tecumseh Sherman in his campaign from Chattanooga to Atlanta, Atlanta to the sea and on through the Carolinas. It was at the Battle of Bentonville, North Carolina, that Nugent lost his right arm while advancing with the firing line, having taken the place of a sick comrade.

More to the point, Nugent was also an experienced attorney. Following the war, he attended Lawrence University and graduated successfully. Nugent studied law under Judge George Baldwin (a multimillionaire and former mayor of Chilton) and Judge Thomas Lynch of Calumet County, and he was admitted to the bar in 1876. By 1884, he had been elected to the position of district attorney of Calumet County but came to Kaukauna in 1889 to be the city's attorney. In June 1894, it was thought that Nugent would move away from the city because he had sold his library and office

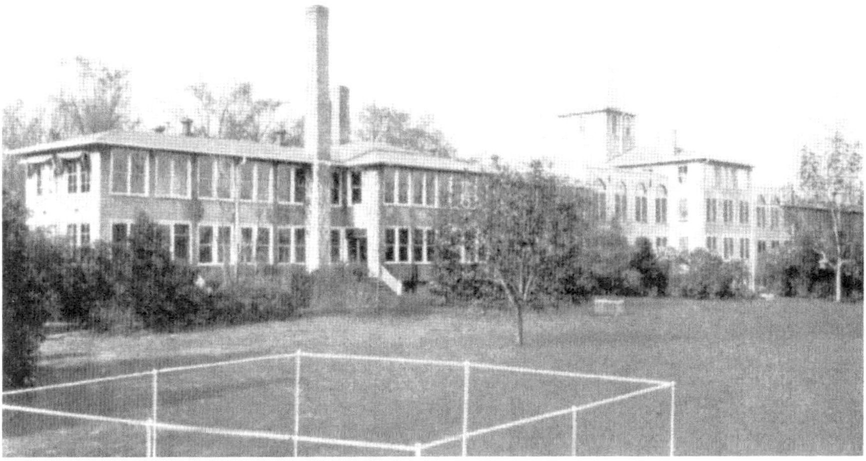

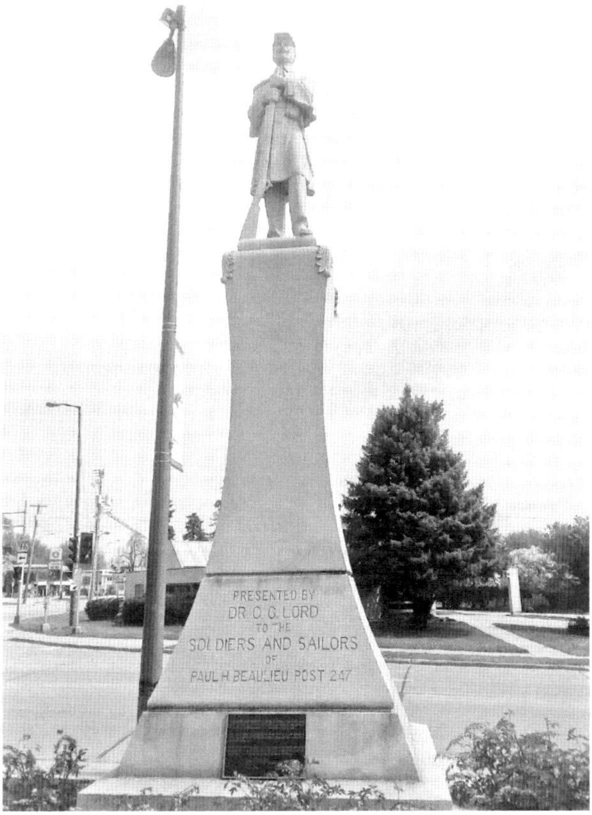

Above: Riverview, the Kaukauna-area tuberculosis clinic set up by Dr. Boyd. *Kaukauna Public Library*.

Left: A statue donated to Kaukauna by Dr. Lord honoring the veterans of the Civil War. *Author's collection*.

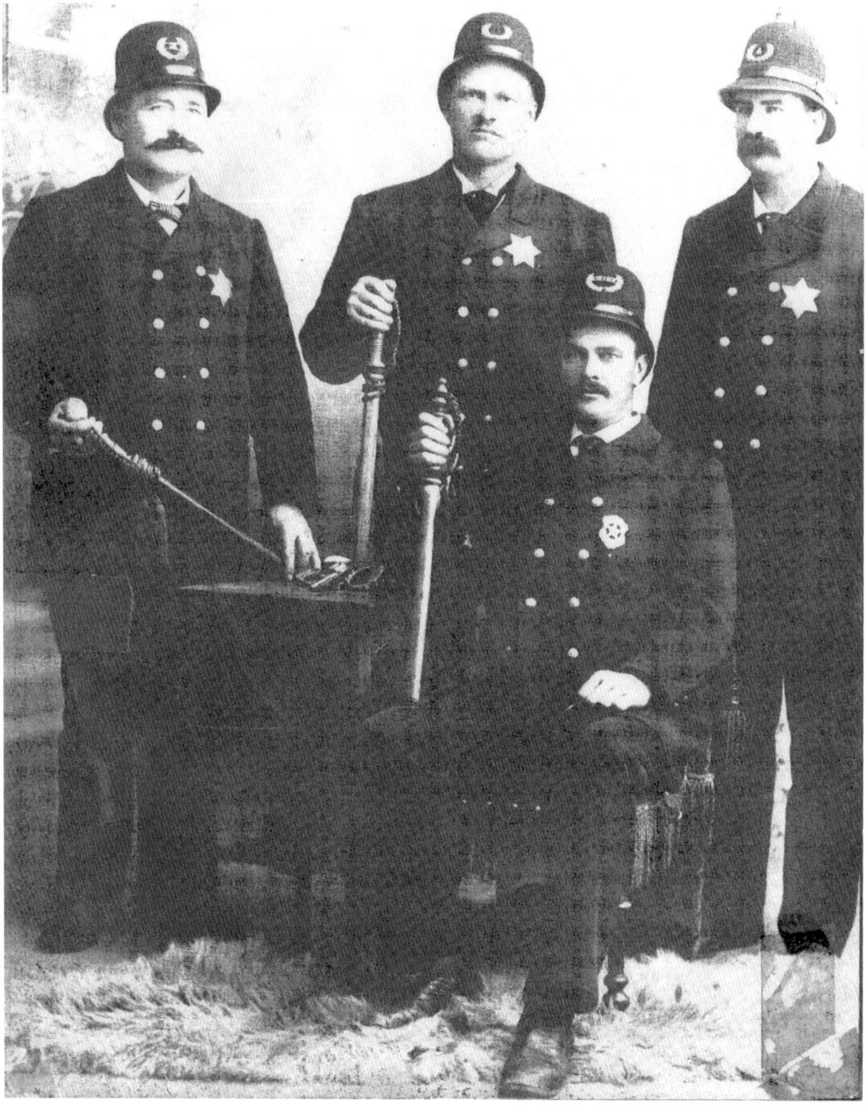

Unidentified Kaukauna police officers showing off their turn-of-the-century uniforms. *Lyle Hansen.*

furniture to fellow attorney Hampton Corlett, but this was simply a minor setback to Nugent's continuing legal career.

Also present was District Attorney John Bottensek on behalf of the state. Bottensek was born in Waukesha County on January 4, 1850, to John Henry Bottensek (an immigrant from Hanover) and Sophia Remmers

Bottensek. In 1855, he moved with his family to Dale and farmed with his father until the latter's death in 1865. John remained on the farm with his mother, brother August and sister Lena (Mrs. Edward Wege) until 1873. John, like Alfred Nugent, graduated from Lawrence University, and the two were equally balanced opponents. John married Elsie M. Buck on September 26, 1878, and together they had a daughter, also named Elsie. The Bottensek residence served as Hamar Union, the student union for Lawrence University, from 1926 to 1951. The building was razed in 1960, and Plantz Hall is now on the site.

Porter Ross was officially charged with the murder of his wife, Nellie Ross, and the case was adjourned until nine o'clock the next morning (along with the jury). Phillip Brown was held over as a material witness with a bond of $200. He was arrested and placed in the lockup, but Appleton relatives posted his bond.

Before sundown, Ross was visited at the jail by a reporter from the *Kaukauna Sun*. Ross was alleged to have lamented, "My poor Nellie; her soul is in hell, and I sent her there." But he was also quick to modify the story in his favor, trying to convince the reporter that Katie was carrying a concealed dirk (a type of sheathed dagger) and that he was only acting in self-defense. Unfortunately for Ross, no knife was found—nor did anyone recall spotting one.

He was also visited that evening by a reporter from the *Appleton Crescent*, who was told of Porter's attempt to starve himself. He would not eat or drink anything offered to him by the officers. "No, I can't do that. I am sustained by other influences." The reporter discovered that Porter was a spiritualist and intended to kill himself in order to meet up with his wife in the near future. When he was asked if her spirit blamed him for what he had done, he said, "No, she had been told of it before hand." Porter further explained that he had often talked with his deceased father through the powers of spiritualism and had been warned in advance that he would someday commit such a heinous act as the one he had accomplished that day. He even claimed he knew that his wife would come to Kaukauna this day and had told his daughters so.

"Do you excuse yourself through spiritualism for shooting the Duprey girl?" he was asked. "No, I am sorry for that," was his reply. "They say she will die but I hope not so she will be able to profit by her experience and be an example to others." Porter's exact thoughts on how this experience would help her "profit" were not clearly established. Porter offered to write a full confession if his lawyer would allow him to do so. When told that he would

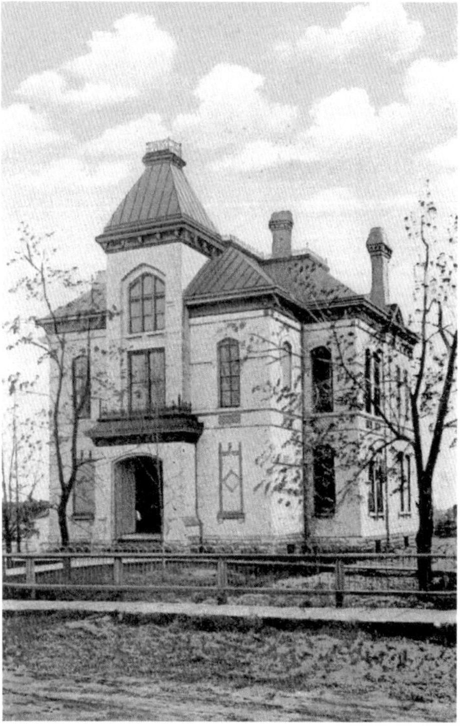

Left: The Calumet County Courthouse in Chilton. *Keith Vincent.*

Below: Lawrence University's Hamar Union, which has since been razed. *Appleton Public Library.*

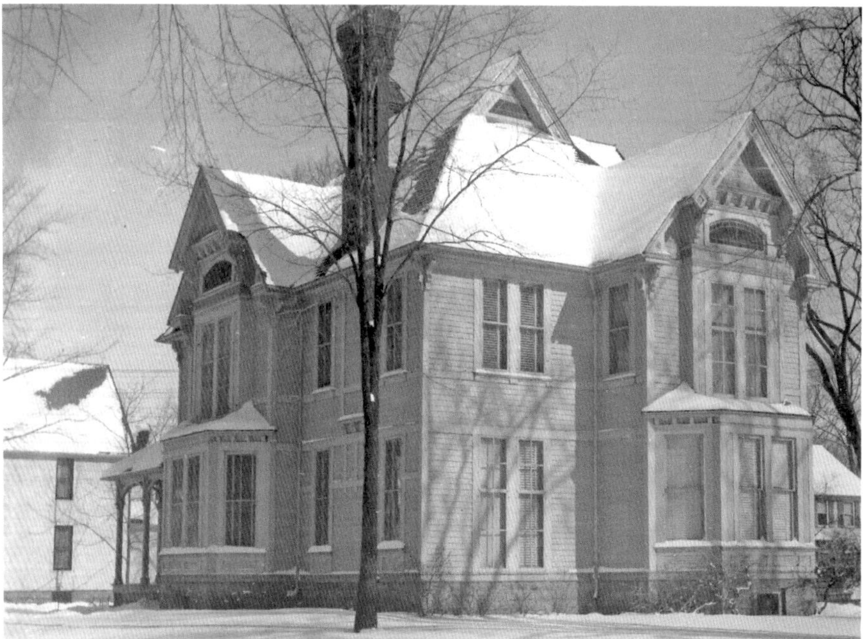

have no strength to write without food, he retorted, "Oh, no! I need no food, for the spirit sustains me and I can do without [food] for forty days."

That night after the reporters left, Porter Ross was visited in his cell by the ghost of his murdered wife. The two of them held hands, and he promised to join her in death after she asked it of him. Numerous guards witnessed this exchange (although they could not see Mrs. Ross) and thought of the "conversation" as particularly queer.

By today's standards, the events inside that jail cell may sound strange or seem to be the sign of a delusional man. But, in fact, the views expressed were not uncommon at the turn of the twentieth century. During the Abraham Lincoln presidency, séances were said to have been performed in the White House by the First Lady. Even in Wisconsin, the movement took hold; no less a figure than Wisconsin governor Nathaniel Potter Tallmadge provided an appendix to John Worth Edmonds's groundbreaking, one-thousand-page magnum opus *Spiritualism*. Another towering Wisconsin figure, Appleton's own Harry Houdini, was a one-man wrecking ball in the world of spiritualism, exposing many psychics and mediums as frauds. Houdini chronicled his debunking exploits in his book *A Magician among the Spirits*, a publication that cost him his friendship with Sherlock Holmes creator Arthur Conan Doyle, a true believer in the psychic world.

Fred Schabo was taken before Judge Mitchell on Tuesday morning after being charged with assault and battery. Schabo was bound over in the sum of $100 for his appearance at the March 12 trial that Friday. The coroner's jury was also asked to reach its verdict by Friday regarding the cause of Nellie's death. The deadline of Friday was given under the belief that Katie would soon pass on.

That afternoon, Chief Reardon attempted to get a statement from Katie Duprey, who was still in horrible shape. She was barely audible, and he could hardly make out what she said, although she confirmed that Porter was indeed trying to kill them. She told Reardon of a letter in which Porter threatened to kill her. The letter, allegedly in a trunk in Appleton, never surfaced to my knowledge.

Reardon also interviewed Porter's maid, Bertha (or Gertie) Mills of Shawano, who told a tale of just how awful she found him to be. The chief determined that Porter was leaving behind a family "in destitute circumstances." I am unable to ascertain what became of any of them while their father was away. Presumably, they were taken in by grandparents.

March 12 came quickly and, at nine o'clock in the forenoon, the coroner's jury declared that Nellie had died "from a shot fired by Porter Ross." The

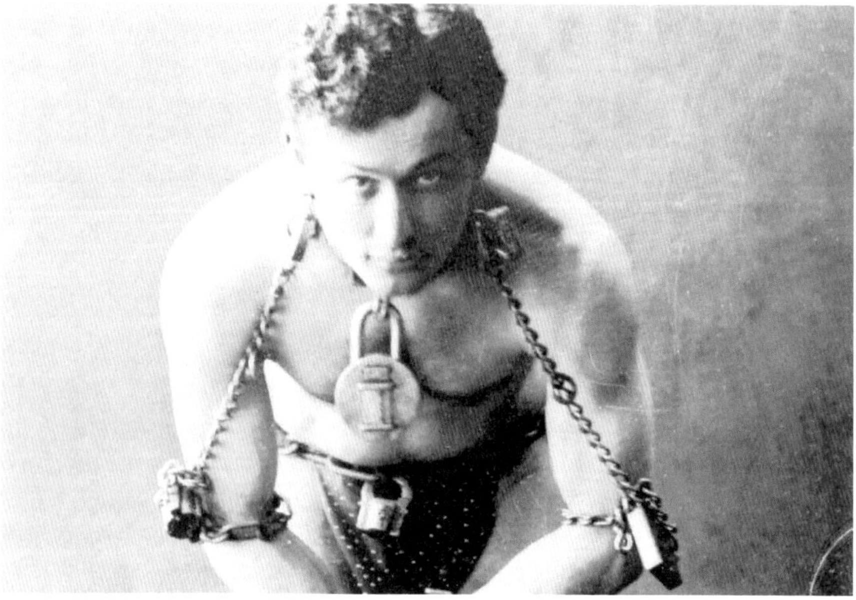

Magician and escape artist Harry Houdini, a skeptic of the spiritualist movement. *Author's collection.*

official matter settled, the remains of Mrs. Ross were boxed up and sent to her father's home in DePere on the noon train.

When the *Kaukauna Sun* was published around noon that same day, readers were greeted by a story in which the *Sun* called for Porter to be punished to the fullest. Included in the article was the cold and callous claim that death "is too good for him; the jail during the balance of his life and hell hereafter will not be sufficient to satisfy justice for his crimes." The March 12 *Kaukauna Times* came to a similar conclusion, stating that it "regret[s] that there was not another bullet in the gun when he placed it to his own worthless head."

The preliminary hearing was held on Saturday morning, March 13, at Heindel's Hall, with Judge Mitchell presiding. Heindel's, situated upstairs from the Bank of Kaukauna, was a venue of many uses; besides court hearings, school commencements and card tournaments were held there. The courtroom scene was quite a spectacle, with "several hundred" people gathered around to hear what the witnesses would say and to catch a glimpse of Porter Ross. The population of Kaukauna at this time was a solid 5,200. The witnesses' testimony was more or less accurate to the story outlined above, with some minor changes or additions worth noting.

1. It was revealed that Louise Beaulieu had already known Katie Duprey, and that the girl had actually worked for her about six weeks in early 1896. The other three people in the sleigh were unknown to her. Beaulieu testified that she had only heard three of the five shots fired. She also added that, besides the witnesses identified in the newspaper, her son Fred Beaulieu was out back carrying in wood at the time of the incident.

2. Amelia Yetke was sworn in as a witness. Yetke, who had been employed by Beaulieu and lived with her for nearly a year, testified that she was upstairs when the two women and Brown originally came up. She had been in the front room or outside during the scuffle, however, and only came back from the woodshed for the final shot, when she saw Nellie Ross falling over dead.

3. Fred Schabo's testimony was consistent with the story. He simply added that he was not acquainted with the two women by anything other than their first names and that he was not aware that either of them was married. He had only met them in Appleton four days prior to the shooting, although he was quite aware of their "character." Fred also added that he had been drinking before reaching the Beaulieu residence, and both he and Brown purchased a bottle of beer when they arrived, as well.

4. Gertie Mills testified that she had been employed by Ross for two months, having come with him from Menominee. He would say on numerous occasions, "Poor Nellie, I will take revenge on the one that led her astray." Gertie testified that Ross was not in the habit of carrying his revolver with him.

Porter had been calm and collected all morning, glancing around the hall "to see how many he knew in the assemblage." However, when Gertie took the stand, he began to cry. While looking at her, he shook his head over and over again.

When court adjourned, Porter asked permission to talk to Gertie Mills. Permission was granted, and he went over to her, saying, "Gertie, I understand you have been telling some terrible stories about me."

A bit flustered, she replied, "Oh, I don't know."

Porter insisted, "Yes, you have. The papers are full of it. Now, for God's sake don't make it any worse for me than it is, you know I have a good deal to stand." He waited a moment and then added, "Gertie, be true to yourself."

Also on Saturday was the case of Fred Schabo's alleged assault and battery. He pled guilty and accepted a sentence of $1.00 and costs, amounting to $6.20 in all.

Court reopened on Monday, March 15, at 9:00 a.m. for the defense to present its case. Attorney Nugent offered no evidence on behalf of his client, and the testimony was closed. The evidence against Porter Ross was found to be sufficient to uphold the charge of murder. Ross was committed to the county jail until the date of his trial. No one had seriously expected the charges to be dropped at this point, and the preliminary hearing was more or less a formality.

Katie Duprey finally succumbed to her ailments on Saturday, March 20.

The weirdness exhibited by the defendant was not exclusive to the city of Kaukauna. On Wednesday, March 31, Porter Ross, while confined at the county jail at Appleton awaiting his trial, called for a doctor during the night. Ross had previously been eating various pieces of tin, but the physician found that he had thankfully given up that habit. Unfortunately, he had "taken to devouring the wire springs of his bed." When Porter told the doctor he had eaten no fewer than sixty pieces of his bedsprings, the bed was thoroughly examined by the guards. Sure enough, they found that a "considerable" amount of wire was missing.

Porter's arraignment before Judge John Goodland finally came on Monday, April 26. He pled not guilty. The docket was a full one. Other

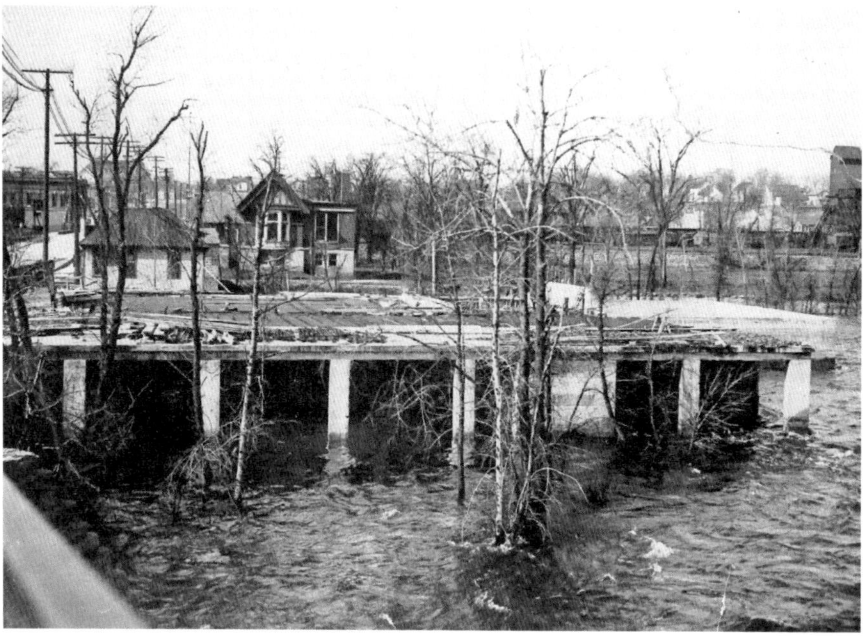

The "foundation of city hall," showing Kaukauna before its municipal building. *Lyle Hansen.*

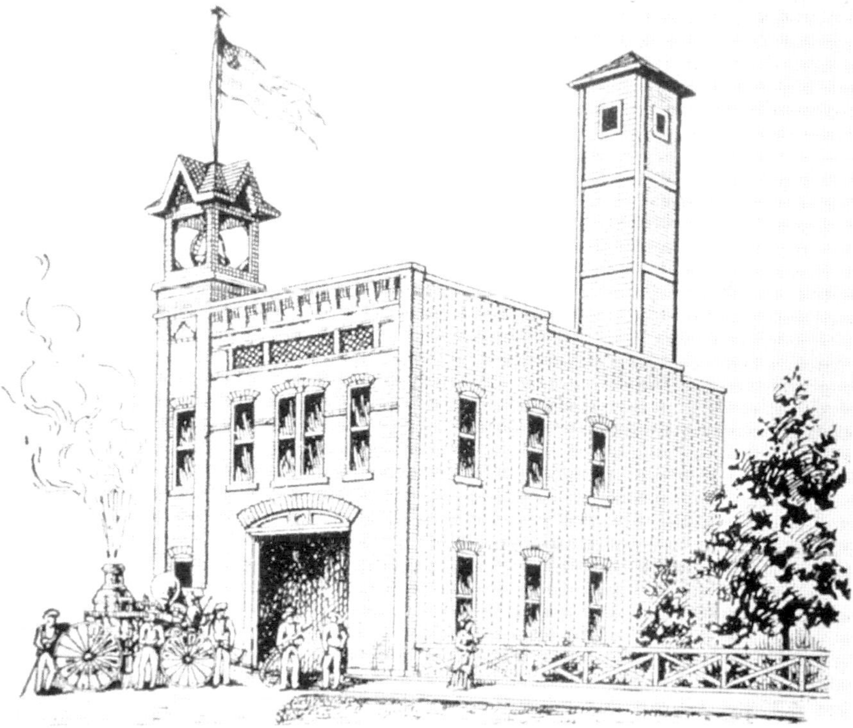

The Kaukauna City Hall as it was roughly in 1891. *Lyle Hansen.*

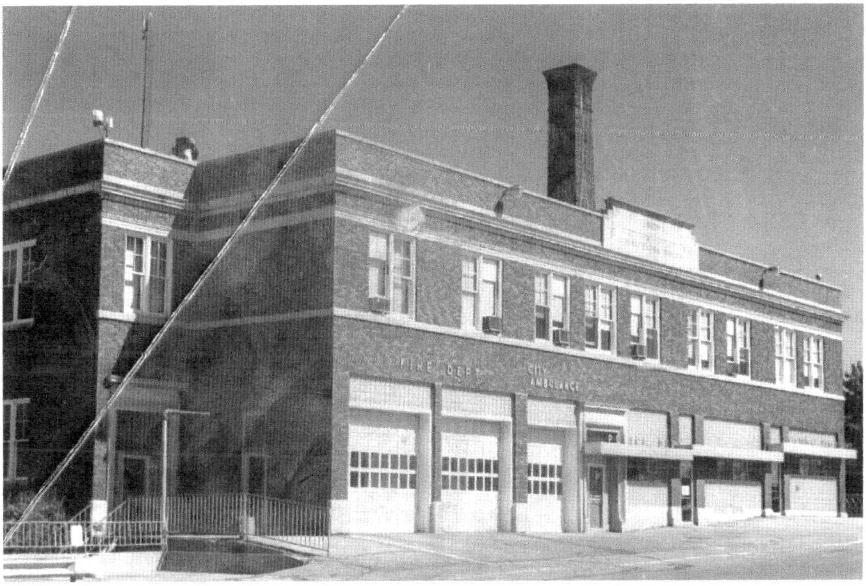

The Kaukauna municipal building as it was for much of the 1900s. *Kaukauna Public Library.*

residents from Kaukauna appearing before Judge Goodland that day included stone quarry foreman Martin Hahn (for forging a $200 note), traveling salesman Sophus B. Morrison (for embezzlement) and former Kaukauna mayor Luther Lindauer (who was suing capitalist Albert Warner Priest for the sum of $150). Defending Ross was, of course, Alfred A. Nugent.

John Goodland may be the most famous and historically important judge in Outagamie County history. Born in England, he came to America as a young man, first driving a butcher's wagon before going on to teach school. He next started a grocery store that was destroyed by fire. Only after these endeavors did he consider the law as a profession, in his mid-forties. Quick to learn, he was elected to the position of district attorney and then circuit court judge in 1891. Goodland signed the paperwork that incorporated Little Chute into the village we know today. His legacy also included two sons, Walter (a future Wisconsin governor) and John (a future mayor of Appleton).

Ross was still being visited in his cell by the ghost of his wife (and now his sister-in-law) as of Monday, May 10. The other jail residents were getting quite upset with what they saw as a "sham of insanity," and Ross succeeded in keeping the sheriff, turnkey and numerous inmates awake for hours on end. To capture the attention of the other jail residents, Ross would shake the gratings, pound the walls and rattle the ventilator until he was sure he had an audience. He would then "flop down" on his cot and begin to talk with "Nellie" and "Katie." When spoken to by others among the living, Porter ignored them and continued to stare straight ahead, sometimes groping at his face and making "dismal" groaning noises. He vowed to get a knife and escape from his cell, joining his wife on the other side.

Sentencing finally came for Porter Ross on Monday, June 21, 1897. In what can only be described as a miracle—or a miscarriage of justice—Judge Goodland sentenced him to a maximum of two years in prison under the charge of fourth-degree manslaughter. The *Kaukauna Sun* was quite upset with the verdict, declaring that if "he had to kill several more the jury would probably purchase the murderer a home and pension him for life." It further said that someone "has failed to do their duty....The blame must fall on the district attorney." According to the paper, numerous witnesses were never called at all, and the evidence—which was quite damning—failed due to this lack.

Before heading off to jail, Ross was re-arrested and charged with the murder of Katie Duprey. The trial would be held when he was released

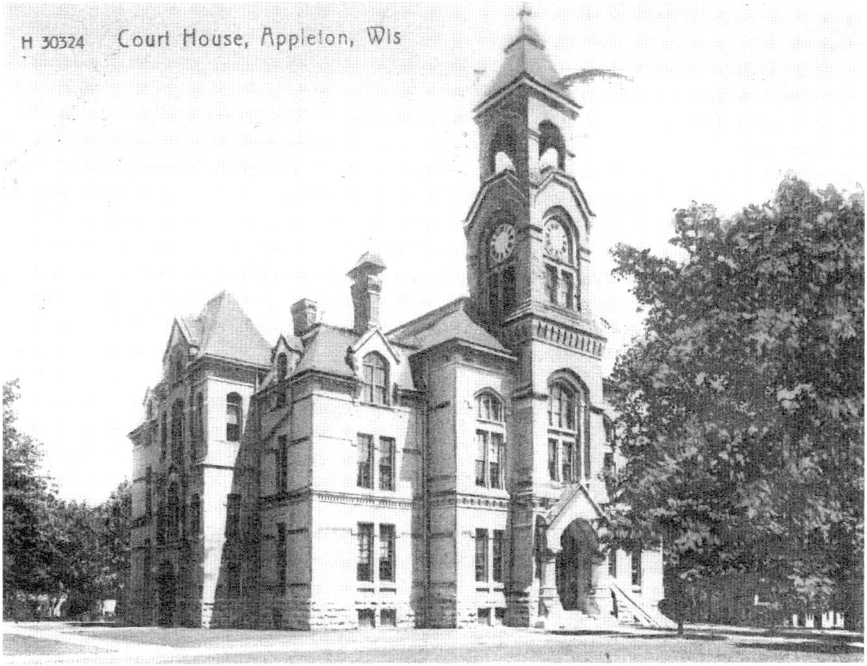

The Outagamie County Courthouse circa 1900, as Porter Ross would have seen it. *Keith Vincent.*

from jail on his current charges. On Tuesday morning, Ross reached the familiar territory of Waupun Prison for the third time in his miserable life. Undersheriff Thomas Mitchell visited Ross (along with prisoners named Sinclaire and Haen) and discovered at that time Ross's prior stays in Waupun and wondered whether that should have played some role in his sentencing from the judge.

After only twenty months, Ross was released from Waupun Prison in March 1899. He had been a model inmate in every sense of the term, according to prison officials. The warden granted him his freedom, along with a new suit of clothes and eleven dollars. This freedom was short-lived, however, because Ross was greeted at the door by Outagamie County sheriff William Wilson and brought back to jail to await his next trial. Wilson was a lifelong public servant in the Republican Party, having previously been Appleton's street commissioner. Ross was arraigned on Monday, April 17, for the murder of Katie Duprey and pled guilty, just as before.

Porter Ross stood trial again on Monday, April 24, 1899, with attorney Nugent defending him once more. A new, young district attorney, Fred M.

Wilcox, was prosecuting. Porter entered the court that afternoon dressed in a plain black suit. Unlike his haggard appearance two years before, Ross now stunned the court, looking even more handsome and younger with his mustache and "chin whiskers." The jail time had taken some life from him, however, as his mustache and hair had both gone quite grey.

Fifty men were drawn up that afternoon for the jury pool, and almost all fifty were called before the court decided on the twelve who would remain. The jury consisted of the following: William Schultz, farmer, of Liberty; Frank Spencer, farmer, of Grand Chute; James McClellon, sawmill operator, of Dale; Horatio Gates Hough, farmer, of Hortonia; William Blake, farmer, of Cicero; Xenophon Earle, pump dealer and inventor of the folding chair, of Appleton; Richard Bottrell, farmer, of Dale; Charles Christenson, farmer, of Maine; Hugh Hagen, farmer, of Greenville; Lewis Cole, painter, of Appleton; Dan Kattke of Appleton; and a twelfth juror inadvertently omitted by the newspaper. Worth noting is the lack of any resident from Kaukauna, Kimberly, Combined Locks or Little Chute—which seems to suggest the bias present in these communities.

The trial resumed the next morning, with attorneys presenting their opening statements. Nugent presented the argument that Ross was justified in his shooting and that the ordeal was an accident resulting from self-defense. The witnesses that morning were Louise Beaulieu, Fred Beaulieu (her son), Dr. Boyd (who tended to Katie Duprey) and Amelia Yetke. Their testimony was substantially the same as it had been in the last trial.

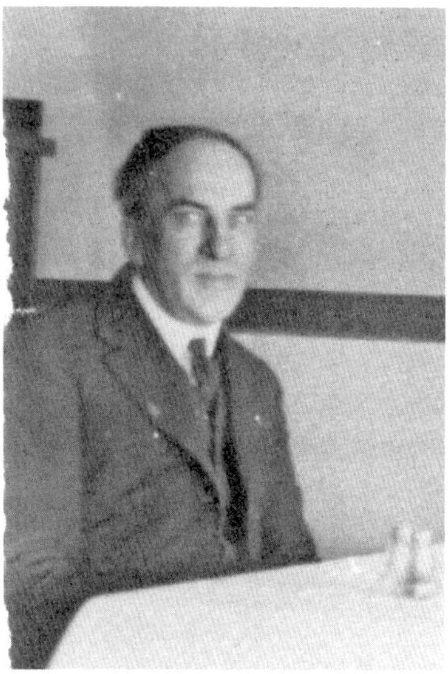

Dr. C.D. Boyd, founder of Riverview and a noted Kaukauna physician. *Kaukauna Public Library.*

The afternoon consisted of Fred Schabo and William Brown (previously identified as "Phillip Brown"), the men who witnessed the shooting. The officers called in to investigate the shooting, Thomas R. Earles and Daniel Reardon, testified. George W. Fargo, the undertaker, also spoke. Katie Ross and Gertie Mills testified, as did several "close relatives" of Katie Duprey. At this point, the state rested.

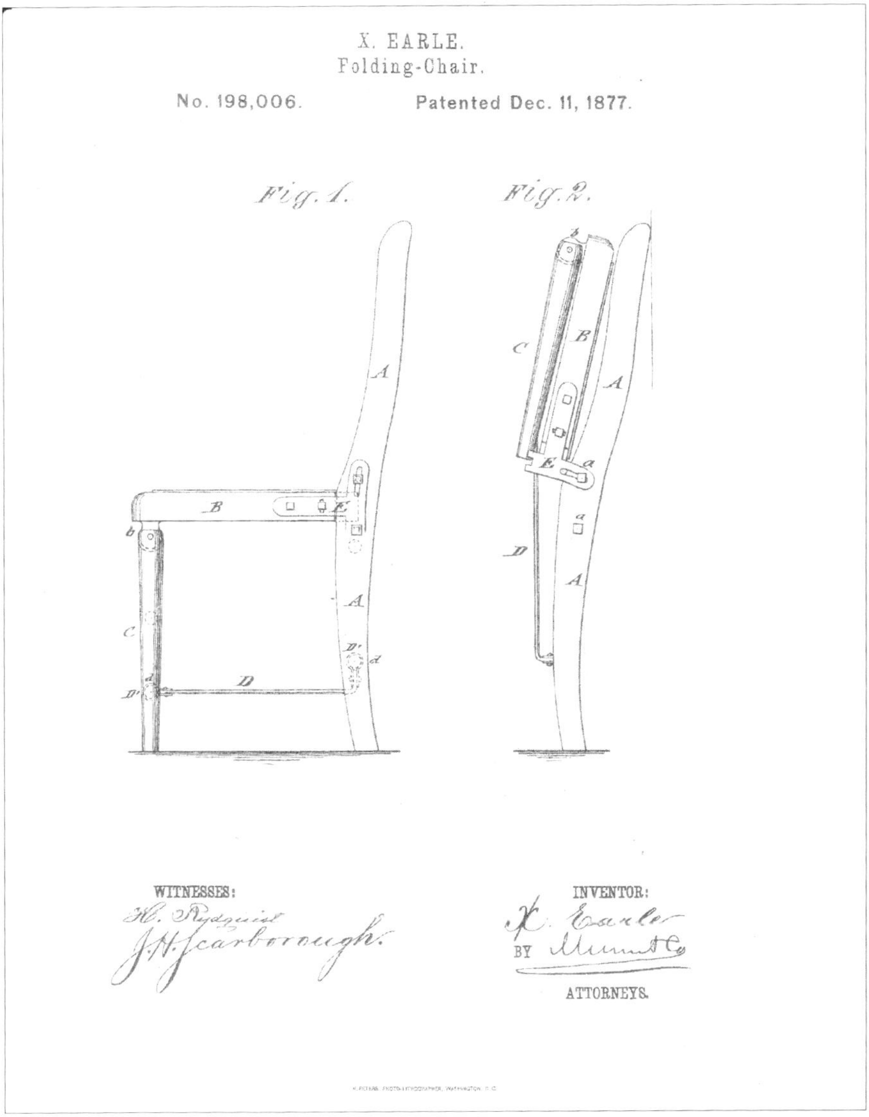

The folding chair as patented by Xenophon Earle. *Author's collection.*

At 10:00 a.m. the following morning, attorney Nugent took up his case. He called on numerous witnesses to show that Porter had a good character and reputation before the shooting incident (which may or may not have been true, as we have seen). Most of the witnesses were residents of Shawano and other communities where Porter lived before Kaukauna. Nugent called Dr.

Frederick Henry Kreiss, who had tended to Porter's injuries in jail. Carrie, Katie and John Ross all testified on behalf of their father. That afternoon, Porter testified that the murders were largely accidental—he intended to shoot only Schabo, but the two women came into the line of fire.

Closing arguments were presented on Thursday morning, April 27. Wilcox spoke "about an hour," and the papers felt he gave "a strong effort." He was followed by Nugent, who "one-upped" him in the eyes of the spectators. He "made a splendid and most convincing speech and was given the closest attention by all in the court room." After lunch, the state closed with a speech from Bottensek, the former district attorney, who also spoke for roughly an hour. At that point, Judge Goodland handed the case over to the jury.

District Attorney Wilcox was apparently no better than his predecessor; after only seventeen minutes of deliberations, the jury believed Porter's story of self-defense. He was acquitted, thus ending what has been called "one of the most sensational and degrading cases ever tried in Outagamie County."

Epilogue

After Porter's trial and acquittal, he was never seen within the city limits of Kaukauna again and was not missed by those citizens. The last reminder of Ross in Kaukauna disappeared in October 1900, when his old house (vacant for three years) burned to the ground. The home, since acquired by the Building and Loan Association, was uninsured and completely unrepairable. As the *Kaukauna Sun* pointed out, the "loss was trifling," a small price to pay to finally be rid of the stench that was Porter Ross.

The family made its mark elsewhere. By 1900, Porter settled in Ironwood, Michigan, and took up work as a carpenter. Porter's daughter Carrie married George J. Wesinski on August 7, 1903, in Hurley, Wisconsin (just over the border from Ironwood). On December 18, 1907, Porter Ross died in Bessemer, Michigan, at the age of sixty-five with few mourning his passing. What became of the Wesinski family or any other Ross descendants is not known.

Epilogue's Epilogue

For those of you who remain curious, Louise Beaulieu did eventually see her day in court. After an unidentified Kaukauna man complained, Sheriff Thomas Mitchell and Deputy P.G. Sherman arrested Beaulieu and three girls living with her on July 13, 1903. One of the women was released, having arrived at the home from Fond du Lac just moments before the bust. The other three were brought before Justice Albert Gustav Koch in Appleton and charged with "keeping and being inmates of a disorderly house." Beaulieu passed in January 1916 at age sixty-six following an attack of "grippe" (influenza).

As for Fred Schabo, the man caught with Porter's wife, he continued his life as a lumberjack, father and grandfather. He was married to Louise Maier at the time of the roadhouse incident. The marriage survived, and Schabo passed away in April 1944.

5

WENZEL KABAT

MURDERER, ESCAPE ARTIST, STATESMAN

The *Kaukauna Sun* called him "a fiend incarnate" who perpetrated "one of the blackest crimes ever committed by a human being." The *Neenah Times* said he was "certainly a degenerate" and "a scamp on general principles" and that he "would steal candy from a child, the molasses from a sick man's ginger cake, or his grandfather's coffin to ride down hill." The *Appleton Crescent* said his actions were "the most horrible crime in the history of Wisconsin." Judge John Goodland declared, "A more heinous crime cannot be found in the history of criminality."

Wenzel E. Kabat was born in Reedsville in roughly 1878. Kabat's father, Joseph, was a wealthy farmer in the Manitowoc area of Bohemian descent. Although Wenzel was the oldest son, he had four older sisters: Mary, Barbara, Rose and Christine. By the time Wenzel reached his teen years, his father had expanded his entrepreneurial ventures to include a successful saloon and hotel that he ran with his wife, Mary Suchan Kabat.

Joseph P. Shimek, a "hotel businessman" of Appleton Junction, was a childhood acquaintance of Wenzel Kabat and gave the following account: "During his school career he was not recognized as an especially docile scholar, but much of his time was taken up at scheming and in devising tricks to play on his fellow schoolmates. The environment in which this boy was reared is not responsible for the way in which he appears to have turned out, for his parents were both honest and conscientious people who always had to work for all they acquired."

The wife of a Kaukauna businessman (name unknown), who attended school with Kabat, had a different story, saying Wenzel "was a bright scholar, the teacher's pet, and always appeared as if he just came out of a bandbox."

At age seventeen, Wenzel attended business college in Chilton. One day, his father came to town and reported the loss of $2,000 in gold that he kept in an old kettle in his cellar. Upon further investigation, it was found that Wenzel had taken the money and used his ill-gotten gains to buy a ticket to go to Milwaukee and attend the state fair.

At age nineteen, Kabat and a man named McGorrow of Green Bay (sometimes referred to as Garrow from Appleton) tried to swindle people, claiming they had perfected a patent on a new cheese vat. Both were arrested but released without trial.

Kabat pivoted from crime to politics. Was this move an attempt to bring him toward respectability? Or was public office just a way to commit crimes by other means? In November 1898, Wenzel ran for the state assembly as a Republican in Manitowoc County. He lost to Canadian-born Democrat Jonas Gagnon, a former tugboat captain, alderman, supervisor and school commissioner from Two Rivers. (Gagnon received 1,881 votes, Kabat 1,404 and Social Democrat Arnold Zander 46.) The newspaper would later report that Kabat "was very active in Republican local party matters, always attending caucuses and conventions of his party and taking much interest in Manitowoc County politics."

Kabat's legend was growing as he seamlessly moved from politics to crime to religion. On May 20, 1899, he was arrested for "false pretenses." Exactly what he did is unknown, but clearly, it was another con. Around 1901, Kabat was studying for the priesthood and was to be ordained, but it was soon discovered that he had broken several rules of the church. The newspapers do not elaborate, but one can speculate about what may have happened. Theft? Lies? Sexual impropriety?

Out of the church, he retreated to crime. Around July 1901, Kabat, with the help of Sheboygan native Herman O. Bornefeldt, forged the names of several Manitowoc and Calumet County farmers in Rockland, Kossuth, Maple Grove, Franklin and Cato to get money. The *Manitowoc Pilot* called this "a slick trick."

These signatures were gathered under the pretense that Bornefeldt was an agent of the German Stock Food Company of Chicago but were instead forged on to promissory notes ranging from $50 to $800, totaling $20,000. Bornefeldt collected the signatures after giving out free samples—he claimed that he needed the signatures to collect his

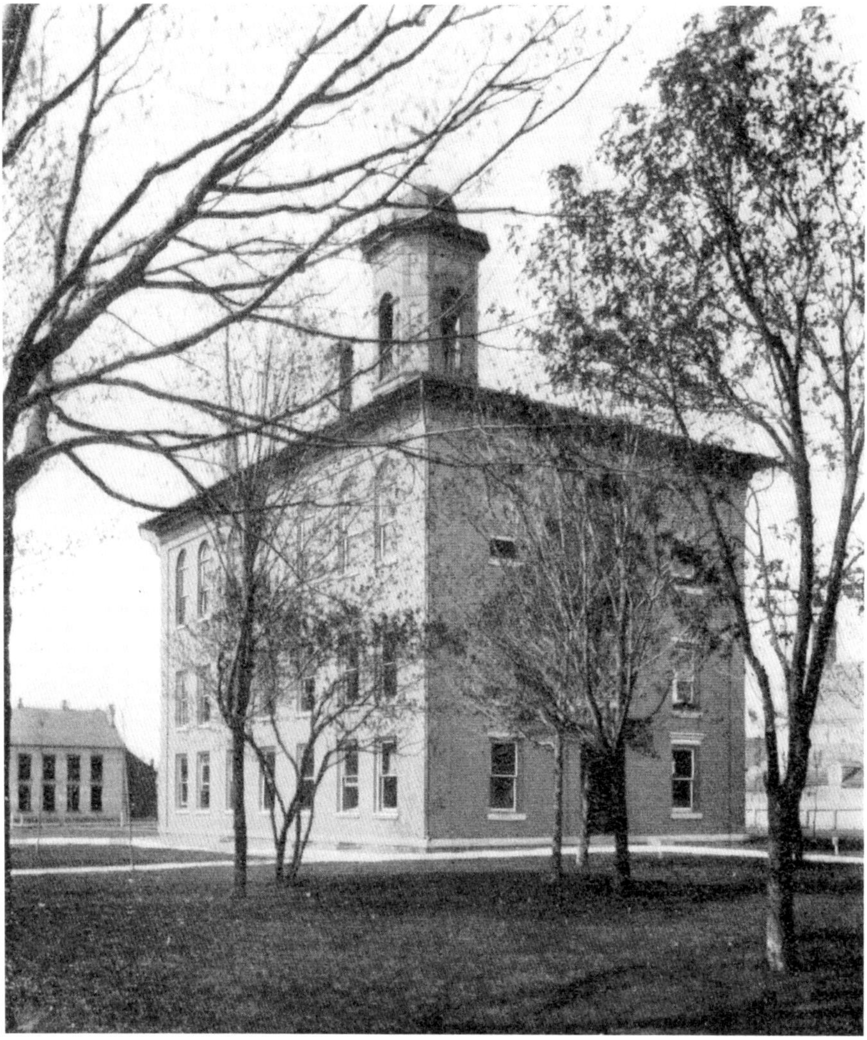

The Manitowoc County Courthouse, as Wenzel Kabat had probably seen it. *Keith Vincent.*

commission. The farmers became understandably upset when asked to pay on the promissory notes that they had not authorized and entered a complaint against Kabat on September 13, 1901. At least thirty of the notes had landed in the hands of a Brillion attorney.

Bornefeldt and Kabat went before the circuit court in the first week of February 1902. District Attorney Albert L. Hougen presented his case for three days, the evidence largely consisting of testimony from the farmers.

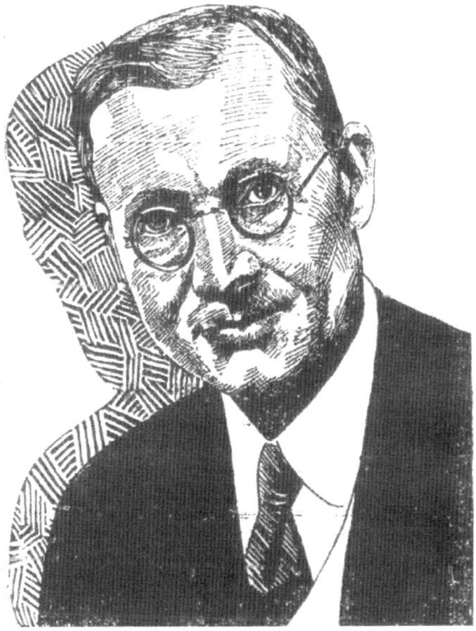

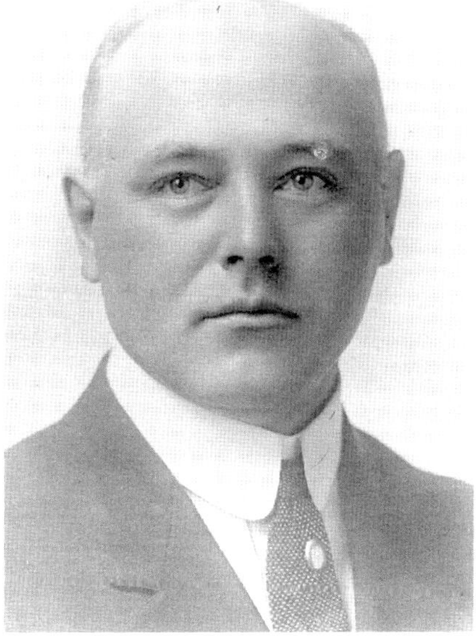

Left: District Attorney Albert Hougen had once successfully put Wenzel Kabat behind bars. *Author's collection.*

Right: Edward Voigt was a defense attorney, though in the Kabat-Bornefeldt trial, he lost his case. *Author's collection.*

Defending the men were George Goodwin Sedgwick (brother of Chief Justice Samuel Sedgwick of Nebraska) for Kabat and Edward Voigt for Bornefeldt. The jury consisted of William Oelrich, farmer John H. Jarr, farmer Charles Pries, wholesale fruit dealer Samuel David Croll, carpenter Mathias Watzel, farmer Emil Kunze, Charles Schultz, farmer Herman C. Wernecke, bank director David William Lorfeld, city hall caretaker Louis C. Geisler, Patrick Kelley and Charles Kiel.

Both men were found guilty of forgery. Their attorneys asked for a new trial but were turned down by Judge Michael Kirwan. By mid-February, Kabat was sentenced to four years in prison and Bornefeldt was sentenced to two. The judge believed that Bornefeldt was a "tool" of Kabat's and not the brains of the operation. Attorney Voigt used the publicity from this case to run for district attorney of Sheboygan County. He won and later ran successfully as the Republican candidate for Congress. Voigt's most notable moment in Washington was voting against entering World War I. As for Judge Kirwan, he was a man who was particularly attached to his community. During the administration of President Grover Cleveland, Judge Kirwan was offered the position of federal superintendent of Indian education, but he declined the office. Twice during his term as circuit court judge, he was offered appointment to the state supreme bench by the governor, but he refused each time, preferring to carry on his work on the circuit bench.

While behind bars, Bornefeldt was a model prisoner and was paroled after one year. After his release from prison, Bornefeldt quickly redeemed himself. Crossing over to Canada, he later enlisted in the infantry in order to fight the German menace in the world war. He was soon gassed while fighting in France and at first was counted among the dead. After a week of despair, his mother, Mathilda, was relieved to find that someone had erroneously put him on the wrong list—Bornefeldt had indeed been gassed but was recovering nicely in the hospital.

Kabat was sent to the Green Bay reformatory but made two escape attempts and was forced to serve the rest of his sentence at the state penitentiary in Waupun. One attempt involved him taking the steel shank from his shoe, sharpening it and using it as a knife to carve a wooden key. These things were discovered while an employee there was making a routine cleaning. Warden Charles W. Bowron was impressed enough by this that he kept the items as a souvenir. Bowron was from Oshkosh and relatively new on the job. James Edmund Heg had resigned as warden in early 1901.

On June 27 or 28, 1905, Kabat was released from the state penitentiary. In July, Kabat hired sixteen-year-old Chester A. Wallen of Green Bay to work for him. Kabat now claimed to be an insurance agent with an office in St. Paul. He also said he had been born in Mexico. After consulting with his current employer, who told him to go for it, Wallen accepted the nonexistent position. Wallen was not the first young man approached by Kabat with the promise of a large salary. Wallen had been working only a few days when he became suspicious of Kabat and left him at Reedsville to work in Manitowoc. Wallen claimed that another young man, twenty-six-year-old Albert Talmadge Hutto, was asked to be a private detective for Kabat. Hutto, a clerk from Manitowoc, declined and went on to work at the Beaumont Hotel in Green Bay, located on the northeast corner of Main and Washington Streets.

At some point in July, during harvest, Kabat was noticed on the McCarthy farm for the first time by fourteen-year-old farmhand Julius Heimke. Heimke, though young, was already a hard worker, as his father was deceased and he needed to support himself and his mother, Minnie. How Kabat came to meet the forty-one-year-old bachelor McCarthy, a man of average build (155 to 160 pounds), is unclear. Kabat, in contrast, was about thirty years of age and rather tall and slim. The farm had been in Michael's possession since June 1899, when he had purchased it from Harriet Pelton Meade.

The *Sheboygan County News* would later report that the land had a dark history. As with all Wisconsin property, it was initially owned by the government. Large patches of land were purchased by Irish immigrant David P. Meade (1790–1857) and his son Captain Matthew J. Meade (1824–1896) between 1850 and 1858. The latter Meade is today a celebrated part of Kaukauna's history, and the Harriet whom Michael McCarthy purchased the farm from was Meade's widow. Matthew Meade's two brothers-in-law, George Lawe and Charles Grignon, are today even more famous, due in no small part to Grignon's mansion becoming a museum.

Michael's sister had previously fallen off a load of hay and broken her neck, dying instantly. In front of the farm was McCarthy Crossing, which was home to several deaths due to passing engines. The first to die was John Yeunger, followed by an Oneida Indian named Peter Smith. An unidentified tramp was killed later, and then John Henry Haas on a Sunday evening in August 1905 had his spine shattered by passing carriages. Between this crossing and Wrightstown had been a number of holdups along the "sand cut"; people feared to travel it at night. Furthermore, Captain William Cogan, watchman of the government dredge, was murdered and burned just down the river from the farm in April 1888. He was initially believed to have suffocated on kitchen stove smoke and burned to death while sleeping, but the dark deed came to light two years later when his watch turned up at an Ashland pawn shop. The watch, unharmed by the fire, was traced to James Graham and Ed O'Deal, who, under questioning, confessed to murdering Cogan, stealing $125 and burning the dredge to hide their crime.

In late August 1905, Michael McCarthy was at Soakup's Saloon in Menasha, where he met auctioneer and real estate dealer John Denhardt

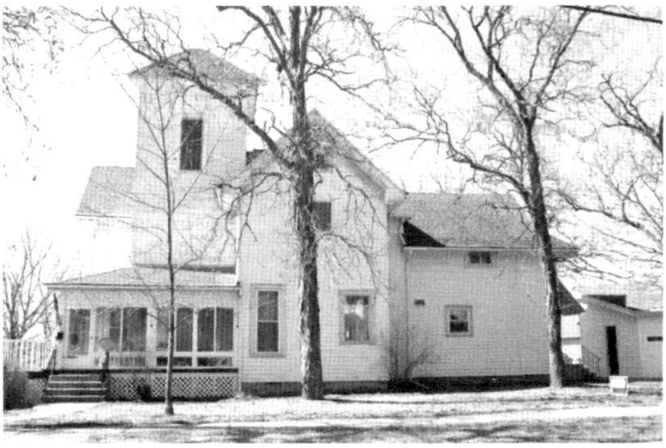

Although Captain Matthew Meade owned much of north Kaukauna, this is the house remembered today. *Author's collection.*

of Winnebago County. They were introduced by a mutual friend, a police officer named Henry A. Bando of Neenah. McCarthy told Denhardt that he was hoping to get rid of his farm within six days so he could use the money to get his eyes fixed in Milwaukee and then visit relatives in Kansas and Nebraska. Michael wrote a description of the Kaukauna farm on the back of a blank milk sheet.

At some point around September 6, Kabat went to attorney George A. Trayser of Kaukauna and offered him $500 to acknowledge a deed. Kabat told him, "I have a friend down in Manitowoc County who has gotten into some trouble with a woman and wants to get away and I am trying to help him." Trayser told him to bring in the friend. "Oh, he won't come," said Kabat. "He does not want to appear in the matter at all. But there will be no trouble about it whatever, for he wants to get out of the country and will never come back." Trayser turned the offer down but did provide Kabat with a list of other attorneys in the area.

Attorney Claude George Cannon of Appleton was asked to help look up records of the McCarthy house, and such information was given. Other statements Kabat made aroused Cannon's suspicion, and he refused to work with him any further. Insurance agent Casper R. Miller of Appleton was approached on the pretext of buying an automobile. During the conversation, Kabat asked Miller if he wanted to make $8,000 or $9,000, and Miller suspected some sort of fraud. He asked how, and Kabat said, "I am going to get some property from a dead man and I want you to help me in the matter. It will be an easy job and no danger of detection. If anyone gets caught at the game it will be myself and you will run absolutely no risk."

Next, Kabat tried to have McCarthy arrested under false pretenses so he could take over the farm. He approached two Green Bay women and asked them to allege that McCarthy had assaulted them. Then an acquaintance of Kabat's, printer Louis E. Root of Green Bay, would appear with a fake badge and a forged warrant and have McCarthy taken to jail. Root was offered $5,000 but turned the money (and the job) down.

Mrs. George Puehler was allegedly assaulted by Michael McCarthy on September 9 in her home on Thirteenth Avenue in Green Bay between 7:00 and 8:00 p.m., and she would later testify to this. She also claimed that Michael had paid her $200 to keep the assault quiet. The whole incident is questionable, because Puehler was a known associate of Kabat, and at the time of the alleged assault at least four witnesses saw Michael at another location in Green Bay. Could they have been mistaken on the exact time? Puehler, by the way, was the niece of attorney Henry

Fitzgibbon. Readers may recall Fitzgibbon as the defense attorney in the George Hammer case; they may be interested to know that he went on to a more distinguished career as a city attorney, a district attorney and even briefly the mayor of Menasha.

A Mrs. Elworth, who lived on Lawe Street north of Holy Cross Cemetery, kept house for McCarthy from time to time. Around Monday, September 11, she was on the farm and agreed to come back on Saturday to help Michael with digging his potatoes.

On September 13, Kabat and Mrs. George Puehler visited the McCarthy farm and departed, with Kabat getting off in Wrightstown and Puehler continuing on to Green Bay. The conductor of this car was Julius Sloth. Michael McCarthy later put on his best suit of clothes and told a fourteen-year-old farmhand named Julius Heimke that he would be going to Wrightstown. Heimke left the farm at 7:30 p.m., and McCarthy was still getting ready. McCarthy would never make it to Wrightstown, as Kabat returned and shot him with his pistol.

On September 14, Kabat was seen by Heimke at 7:00 a.m., when the boy arrived. The man was inside washing the milk and cream separator. He then took McCarthy's clothes, underwear, stockings and shoes and moved them in to the woodshed. Kabat was later burning brush shortly after 8:00 a.m. As Heimke approached the fire, Kabat sent him away. That morning, a neighbor boy saw Kabat bring brush to a pile, and other neighbors saw him bring old boards and fence posts to the brush pile, which was "burning furiously." Farmer Charles Quigley of Lawrence was riding the interurban car from Green Bay to Kaukauna and from his seat could see the fire between 7:00 and 8:00 a.m.

Heimke further saw Kabat take a pearl-handled revolver out of a drawer that Heimke had never seen before and was then offered a gold watch that he knew to be McCarthy's.

A bill of sale dated September 14 was made up in the office of attorney (and former judge) Lafayette A. Calkins of Green Bay but not signed there, and Calkins claimed no knowledge of any plot.

On Friday, September 15, Anthony Reith, a fourteen-year-old boy, was rabbit hunting with his dog when he found a pool of blood in a secluded place near the river on McCarthy's farm. The dog smelled the blood and became frightened and ran home. On the farm was a saw covered in blood and human hair, and Reith hid it in a hollow tree, thinking the tool might be useful sometime. Walking over a hill, he saw Kabat burning brush but didn't trust him, so Reith returned home. The next day, he came down with smallpox. The fire was estimated to have burned seven oak trees and multiple cans of kerosene. Also witnessing the fire on September 15 were John Krull and Joseph Diers of Kaukauna, two boys who were gathering hickory nuts. When they saw the fire, it was about four feet high.

That same afternoon, Kaukauna junk dealer Isaac Ginsburg of the Saving Center Store stopped by the farm and purchased some scrap iron from Kabat. He also helped load up some cattle, which they brought and sold to butcher Frank Ehnerd. Kabat told both men conflicting stories about McCarthy—Ginsburg was told that Michael had moved to a farm up north, while Ehnerd was told that Michael was merely away at the state fair in Milwaukee.

Mrs. Elworth returned on Saturday, September 16, to dig potatoes but found Kabat on the farm rather than McCarthy. She noticed he had scrubbed the kitchen floor. Kabat did not take a liking to her and instructed Julius Heimke to shoot her with a rifle if she ever returned to the property. About this same time, Edward and William Terry were picking hickory nuts when they found a lantern on McCarthy's farm and put it in the hickory bag. They also saw Kabat on the property talking to other men they did not know, presumably about selling off the stock.

Kabat sold more cattle on September 20, this time to Robert Ehnerd. He also sold two colts, which Ehnerd immediately sold to another person and made a five-dollar profit.

On Sunday, September 24, Kabat took an interurban car from Kaukauna to Green Bay with Richard McCarthy, and they talked at length. At some point, Charles McCarthy went to 220 South Quincy Street in Green Bay to talk to Elizabeth "Lizzie" Merritt, wife of shipping clerk William Morris Merritt. She may have had some valuable information, but McCarthy received little satisfaction when she told him that Michael had just left. In fact, Merritt had never met Michael at all but was instructed by Kabat to say he "just left" if anyone ever inquired about his whereabouts.

Charles McCarthy was intercepted by Kabat, who told him that Michael had gotten into trouble by following a woman to her home, throwing her down and choking her. He was hiding out in a boardinghouse, and Kabat took Charles there, but the doors were locked. Kabat next took Charles to the fair and treated him royally, claiming they might find the woman there or Michael in disguise. Kabat then accompanied Charles back to the car to Kaukauna. The McCarthy relatives doubted Kabat's story of Michael assaulting a woman and had him turned in to authorities when it became clear that Michael was not coming back. At this point, it is worth reminding readers that Charles McCarthy had previously crossed paths with another killer, Porter Ross. He had now looked into the face of evil twice!

District Attorney Albert H. Krugmeier and attorney T.H. Ryan had Kabat in the "sweat box" for nearly four hours, but he refused to give the assaulted woman's name or divulge McCarthy's whereabouts. For the time being, he had to be released. Krugmeier was born in Minnesota, the son of William and Dora Krugmeier, who moved to Dodge County, Wisconsin, soon after his birth. Krugmeier attended school at Horicon, and after graduating there he entered the University of Wisconsin Law School, earning his law degree in 1898. He located at Appleton for the practice of his profession and by dint of hard study and labor began to enjoy a good practice. In 1905, he was elected to the office of district attorney for Outagamie County. Whatever time he could spare from his law practice he devoted to a dairy farm located just outside of the city of Appleton. The farm was a model of cleanliness. Krugmeier, politically, was a Republican and served two terms as chairman of the Republican County Committee.

On Monday, September 25, Marshal Richard Conlon, who had known Michael for twenty-five years, went to Green Bay and played the role of detective, talking to a woman of interest, most likely Lizzie Merritt. She admitted Michael McCarthy had been there but claimed she had no part in his disappearance. Conlon took up lodging for the night in a private boardinghouse, claiming to be a collector from Chicago.

Conlon called on Kabat's sister, claiming to be a man disposing of real estate on his way to the Pacific coast. She informed him that Kabat was not there and that she did not know where he was.

He next wrote a "decoy telegram," telling the delivery boy to strike a match if Kabat was home so the officers could swoop in and make an arrest. The lady answering the door said he had been there for supper but had left to go to the theater. Conlon then scanned the local vaudeville theater and did not find Kabat. He continued his search in Green Bay at various saloons.

Tuesday, September 26, 1905, at about 6:00 a.m., Kabat was arrested by Marshal Conlon. Conlon and another man went to the house where Kabat was staying, with the man guarding the back door to prevent Kabat's fleeing. Without Conlon even knocking, Kabat came out and was surprised to find Conlon in front of him. Kabat asked if Conlon had a warrant—he did not. After some insistence, Kabat was taken back to Kaukauna regardless of the warrant. He was allowed to take with him a roll of bills, which amounted to several hundred dollars.

Conlon and Richard McCarthy had a long interview with Kabat, lasting approximately four hours, but failed to get anything out of him. He repeatedly contradicted himself or would change the subject on a whim. That same afternoon, Kabat was arraigned before Justice Nic D. Schwin on the charge of "kidnapping" Michael McCarthy, as no corpse could be found. The *Kaukauna Times* reported that the proceedings "were the strangest ever recorded in this part of the state." His examination was postponed until the following Monday, and he was committed to the county jail in Appleton due to his failure to pay the $1,200 bond.

Kabat secured Albert M. Spencer of Appleton as his attorney. Spencer was born in Bovina Township, Outagamie County, the son of Blanchard and Emily Curtis Spencer. Blanchard Spencer came from New York to Wisconsin in 1850, where he engaged in the lumber industry. After attending the public schools, Albert went to the Ryan High School and then read law under Judge Joseph E. Harriman and Sloan & Bottenscher, being admitted to the bar in 1883. During the next year, he was elected to the office of district attorney and was reelected in 1886, but he retired from that office in 1887 and went to Superior, Wisconsin, where he remained for eight years. In April 1896, he returned to Appleton and served in the office of city attorney for three terms after having taken a trip through Colorado and Arizona. Albert's son Harold Spencer was notable as a midshipman in Annapolis, Maryland, connected with the United States Diplomatic Service in Africa.

The young Julius Heimke, who worked on McCarthy's farm, was questioned in connection with the case, as he now possessed McCarthy's gold watch and rifle. He falsely claimed the items were gifts from McCarthy and said he knew nothing of the disappearance.

On Thursday, September 28, 1905, an unidentified woman went to the county jail asking to conduct an interview with Kabat. She was accompanied by a Kaukauna girl who was stopping with her brother on the McCarthy farm. The interview was granted, and after it was over, the woman took the girl to Kamps and Sacksteder's drugstore, where they purchased an ice cream soda. Together, they took a car to the North Western depot, where they separated.

Marshal Conlon and Sheriff Albert G. Koch followed the woman to Green Bay and again to the outskirts of the city. (Sheriff Koch is the same man mentioned as a justice of the peace in our preceding chapter.) They waited across the street while she was in a restaurant and then trailed her to the house where Kabat had been arrested and, still farther, to the boardinghouse where Conlon had boarded the night of Kabat's arrest.

They secured the woman's name from the Kaukauna girl and returned to investigate on September 29.

At some point, Marshal Conlon was able to interview the mysterious woman. She claimed to have met Kabat five years prior (in 1900) in Milwaukee and had known him ever since. She was not aware that McCarthy was missing and was informed of this. She then said bluntly, "I wonder if Kabat killed him." She further admitted having had trouble with McCarthy but said it was some time ago and amounted to nothing. She visited the McCarthy farm in Kabat's company on one occasion but made no demands of the owner. The woman, never identified by the press, was about twenty-four years old and married.

The woman and her husband joined Marshal Conlon at the district attorney's office in Appleton, where she was interviewed by the DA and attorney T.H. Ryan. Apparently, much valuable information was secured, and a suitcase containing papers and other property belonging to Kabat was handed over to authorities by his sister. The grip contained "much incriminating evidence," including a bottle of carbolic acid (phenol) and some "knock-out drops." Several packets of McCarthy's papers were found, including letters, receipts, cancelled notes and the deed to the Kaukauna farm. Also inside were a revolver, a pair of handcuffs, poker chips, "a stick of dope," a pocket knife and a Pinkerton detective star.

Not found in the grip was a deed to a 640-acre farm that McCarthy had owned in Mirage, Nebraska, since roughly 1889. A letter was found, though, that placed the value of the land at $50 per acre, or $32,000. Investigators suspected that Kabat may have already sold that second property. The precise location of the Nebraska farm is unclear. It was reportedly in Sheridan County, in the north of Nebraska. Mirage last appeared in the census in 1910, and the farm's exact location today is not known. I believe it would be a few miles south of Hay Springs.

District Attorney Krugmeier visited Milwaukee with the bill of sale and several examples of McCarthy's penmanship. After consultation with handwriting expert John Fawcett Tyrrell of Milwaukee, the bill was quickly determined to be a forgery. Tyrrell's career highlights were yet to come—he would later be an expert witness for the Leopold and Loeb trial, as well as in the Lindbergh baby kidnapping case. A representative of the *Kaukauna Sun* also examined the bill of sale and compared the signature ("M.M. Mc.Carthy") to that of other samples from McCarthy ("M M McCarthy"). He quickly judged it a forgery, as the *M*s were different, there were periods after the Ms (which Michael did not use) and there was even a period after the Mc, which no person whose name starts with "Mc" would ever do.

On Saturday, September 30, there was a rumor going around that McCarthy's head had been found in some bushes near a riverbank in Wrightstown. Police found no foundation for these claims. The next day, approximately fifty people met at the McCarthy farm to search for Michael's body. A pair of sleeve garters was found some distance from the house, partially burned. The name "M.M. McCarthy" was found written on the side of the house several times, as though someone was practicing the signature. Inside the house, a bottle of ink and a pen were found that matched the color of the ink used on the bill of sale.

On Monday, Kabat appeared before Justice Schwin at 10:00 a.m., and his bond was raised from $1,200 to $2,000, which he could not pay. The examination was postponed until Wednesday, October 11, because Kabat's attorney, Albert Spencer, had been called to Grand Rapids on business. A large crowd had gathered in the court and outside, and rumblings of people calling for a lynching were evident. Kabat feared violence when he was escorted back to the interurban car by Sheriff Koch, Patrolman Julius Kuehn and Patrolman Hamilton. He made it back to the county jail without incident.

In the jail, he was granted few privileges, and every precaution was taken to prevent his escape. He was not granted newspapers, though he was able to purchase delicacies with his own money, including chicken lunches. He was said to purchase apple pie every night and also loved chocolate. When candy was not provided, "he was very much disappointed," according to the *Appleton Crescent*. He also sat in fear of retribution from McCarthy's friends, many of whom he knew personally.

Over the next several days, rumors circulated in McCarthy's neighborhood that Kabat was a member of an organized band that may be swooping in, killing off people and taking their land. The newspaper reported, "Every home has been converted into an arsenal that bristles with firearms." There was also speculation that Marshal Conlon was being followed by the brigands. One night around eleven o'clock, when his son John came home, he saw a stranger near the window, wearing a brown overcoat and a soft hat. They grappled, but the man escaped and met up with a companion. The marshal was not home at the time.

On Tuesday, October 3, Frank X. Berens was looking around the McCarthy farm in the afternoon and came across the two spots where Kabat had been burning brush. Berens found what he believed to be a bone in the ashes.

On Friday, October 6, Frank Berens returned to the McCarthy farm, this time with Kaukauna saloonkeeper Peter Eimmerman. The pair was in a boat around 3:00 p.m., and when the men reached the McCarthy farm, they decided to go ashore. They were not able to find much, as Kabat had apparently swept the ashes into a wheelbarrow and dumped them somewhere. They did find a partially burned rib bone nearby, though, that had been ejected from the fire. They also found a spot where fresh sod was placed on top of black muck. With sticks, they moved the sod and found a cache of bones. They fetched Marshal Conlon. Altogether, they found part of a skull, pieces of ribs, finger joints, teeth, suspender buckles and shirt buttons. Dr. William N. Nolan of Kaukauna confirmed the bones as human, and Dr. Oscar F. Siekman of Appleton identified the teeth as human, from the upper part of the mouth.

Charles McCarthy, Michael's father, had come under so much stress that he fainted and fell in his home. Until the mystery of his son was solved, he gave up his home in the country and moved to Kaukauna, where he could attend to any business that might arise.

On Monday, October 9, Marshal Conlon and Attorney Ryan visited the McCarthy farm and retrieved the axe and saw that had allegedly been used to kill and dismember McCarthy before his body was burned. They were accompanied by Anthony Reith, who had hidden the saw in a tree. The axe was found nearby in a stump. Reith had just recovered from smallpox and was unable to take them sooner. This same day, George Bombard and Frank Smith of Kaukauna found a three-foot-long pine club with oil and blood stains on the farm, but this did not seem to be connected to the case.

A few days before Kabat's hearing, Peter Eimmerman received a threatening letter in the mail, the envelope bearing the stamp of the railroad post office of the Wisconsin-Michigan division at Ishpeming. The letter advised Eimmerman not to testify at the hearing and to "discontinue to play the role of a Pinkerton." He should "stop meddling in other people's affairs" and "keep his mouth shut or else [the writer would] close it forever." Eimmerman put the letter in a book, but it was later taken by someone prior to October 26. The letter was written in a "running hand," was not dated and was signed with a skull and crossbones.

Kabat's preliminary hearing was on October 11, and he was brought in to Justice Schwin's court by officers Conlon, Kuehn and Hamilton. District Attorney Krugmeier asked the judge to drop the charge of kidnapping, which he did, and then filed a complaint of murder against Kabat. Kabat refused to plead guilty or not guilty, but once Charles McCarthy and Julius

Heimke testified, the charges were set. Several boys sat outside and charged onlookers five cents apiece to glimpse Kabat through the window.

On Friday, October 13, Henry Gloudemans, the former owner of the interurban saloon in Little Chute, moved his family to the McCarthy farm. He hoped to buy the two hundred acres from Michael's estate for $12,000 cash.

Mrs. Dominic F. Pech, the former Rose Kabat and sister of Wenzel Kabat, spoke with a reporter at her home on North Broadway in Green Bay on the morning of October 14 and declared her belief that Wenzel was innocent.

> *He is as tender-hearted a person as I ever knew and I know he did not kill Mr. McCarthy. Why, the relationship between them was too friendly for one thing, and he could not be cruel enough to do such a horrible deed as the papers try to make people think him guilty of. Once, since he has been living with us, we had a sick cat and I asked him to kill it, and if he could not kill an animal, he surely could not kill a human being. Yes, Mr. McCarthy was a frequent visitor at our home, and it appeared to me, at least, that he and my brother were on very friendly terms. His last call was on the "big" day of the fair, and as he walked up onto the porch of our house, he drew a paper out of his inside coat pocket which looked to me like a deed. Mr. McCarthy and Wenzel went into the parlor and there talked about something, the deed I suppose. When they came out there was no sign of any ill feeling.*

Pech suggested that McCarthy might be visiting some relatives out west. Living in the same home as Pech was Mrs. John Balis, who knew nothing.

In the twenty-first century, investigators are blessed with a wide array of forensic science techniques to help catch criminals. Fingerprints, DNA and fiber analysis are some of the more well known. Although television shows such as *CSI* have exaggerated the potential of such evidence, it has been responsible for solving countless crimes that would have otherwise remained unsolved. Unfortunately, in the early 1900s, practically none of these methods were available to detectives.

For example, on October 27, 1905, Professor Marshall Davis Ewell came forward to say that medical science could do very little with blood evidence. "According to the present state of our knowledge, it appears to be settled that the blood corpuscles, even in the fresh state, of man, dog, rabbit, guinea pig, musk-rat, monkey, elephant, lion, whale, seal, otter, kangaroo, wombat and porpoise cannot be distinguished from each other by micrometric measurement….It would be extremely perilous to undertake, by micrometric measurements alone, to distinguish the blood of man from that of another animal."

Strictly speaking, Professor Ewell was wrong. The Uhlenhuth test, or the antigen-antibody precipitin test for species, was actually invented by Paul Uhlenhuth in 1901 and could distinguish human blood from animal blood, based on the discovery that the blood of different species had one or more characteristic proteins. So such a test did, in fact, exist. However, it may be true that it was not yet in wide use or accepted in court. And, even if it was, the day of blood typing was still to come, so attempting to determine whose blood was whose was virtually impossible.

Michael McCarthy's will was admitted to probate on November 2. The handwritten will had been drawn up on December 12, 1894, in Mankato, Jewell County, Kansas. Being outdated, it put the value of the Kaukauna farm at $4,000, and it was now said to be worth $17,000. Likewise, Michael valued his Nebraska farm at $3,000, which was quite low. The will asked that money be given to "the poorest priest" so that he may "say mass for the holy souls in purgatory." To his family, he gave Timothy $700, Dennis $600, Florence $500 and brother Charles $400. He asked that $1,000 "be judiciously distributed amongst the very poor of some large city." Money was also allocated to move his brother Dan's remains from Eston graveyard to Sniderville. Witnesses to the will were William O'Reilly and J.D. Lynn.

As of November 1905, there were only five prisoners in the Outagamie County jail, a place the *Appleton Crescent* dubbed the "Hotel Koch." During the greater part of the day, the prisoners were allowed to be together and walk around in one of the corridors enclosed by steel bars. Kabat was "rather sour looking and is as 'mum as an oyster.' He speaks to no one entering the building. His expression is not pleasant." The other four prisoners were:

1. Thomas "Sleepy Tom" Cahill, a member of the notorious "Boo Gang" in Appleton's Third Ward. He was held on a charge of burglary. He was an Irishman by blood.

2. Elias Cornelius, an Oneida Indian laborer charged with assaulting a "squaw" on the reservation. Cornelius had been known to cry in the jail, being homesick and missing his wife, Annie, and his nineteen-month-old son Aaron in Oneida. He was said to spend his days whistling and moving about. According to the reporter, Cornelius was "good looking" and "well built."

3. Jacob Palm, a Prussian serving sixty days for assault and battery. He had been sentenced by Justice J.H. Cook. Since last leaving the jail in June, Palm had been making his home with relatives in the Fourth Ward, and it was during a quarrel with them that he is said to have made the assault. He was the oldest of the five and said little, his face "practically expressionless." Of the four, Palm was Kabat's least favorite, as he had the habit of "moving the rotary, inch at a time by means of a board," and "the creaking noise almost drove Kabat mad." Palm later died, not surprisingly, in the county asylum.

4. Lai Quen, a Chinese immigrant found guilty of violating the Chinese Exclusion Act, was awaiting deportation. His face was "constantly beaming in smiles while visitors are in the building" and appeared "to be greatly pleased to see people with whom he is acquainted."

During Kabat's stay, the Outagamie County jail was declared "unsanitary as well as unsafe," and those imprisoned there would have to be moved. Sheriff Simpson of Winnebago County consented to take Kabat. An unnamed member of the Outagamie County Board also appreciated this option, as it cost them $28.00 a week to house Kabat in Appleton, due to the extra guards, but it would cost only $4.50 in Oshkosh. In all, the savings was said to be $448.00. On Thursday, November 23, the *Kaukauna Sun* wrote an editorial pleading with Outagamie County not to send Kabat to Oshkosh while the jail was being rebuilt. It preferred he stay there or be sent to Waupun. "By sending a prisoner to another jail, sympathy is apt to take the place of justice and schemes may be hatched to thwart the law rather than to enforce it." The paper asked Judge Goodland to overrule the county board if it decided to send Kabat away. It was possible that Kabat might not have appeared before the same judge as Porter Ross. Goodland's seat for circuit judge came up for reelection in 1903, and he successfully fended off another man we have become familiar with, John Bottensek. The vote was as follows: Goodland (Democrat): 2,831; Bottensek (Republican): 1,243.

On Tuesday, December 12, Outagamie County Judge Kreiss declared Michael McCarthy legally dead; his will was allowed to enter probate. Testimony was taken from Charles McCarthy, Julius Heimke, Thomas H. Ryan and Marshal Conlon. Depositions were taken from William O'Reilly and J.D. Lynn, the men who witnessed the will. Charles McCarthy and Charles Jr. were appointed co-executors of the will.

On Thursday, December 21, August Niennemann arrived at the Outagamie County jail after failing to pay the $500 bond for threatening to kill his wife. Kabat took "much amusement" at hearing Niennemann complain about his situation. After three days, he told Kabat and a guard that he wished to hang himself. The guard told him to cheer up, as he only had 177 days left to serve. "What, me stay here 177 days?" he asked.

"Sure, you have been here 3 days, and that only leaves you 177 more to serve," replied the guard. Niennemann was not cheered by this and eyed up a clothesline for hanging himself in the corridor. Kabat informed him that the line was not heavy enough and directed him to another one. Niennemann spent much time fretting about his life insurance, despite it being only $150, because the benefit would go to his wife. He preferred to sign the policy over to Kabat, the sheriff or a guard. Kabat was said to be "enjoying life" now due to Niennemann's "entertainment."

Kabat's parents visited him in the county jail on Tuesday, December 26. He refused to kiss his mother; when she asked if he was innocent, he told her to go home if she was going to talk about his troubles. He was not full of joy to see them. Kabat's father told the *Kaukauna Sun* that Wenzel "was the black sheep of the family and I cannot do anything with him or for him." He further told the *Manitowoc Daily Herald*, "Instead of getting better he seems to be going from bad to worse. The other five children are all good, but Wenzel has been bad for years. I will not contribute any money toward the defense of my son. I have none too much and I will refuse to squander it in a cause that may net nothing. My son should have profited by his former arrest and imprisonment, and now be as good a boy as when he was 13 years old, but he has gone from bad to worse. No one can feel the horror of the affair like my wife and myself." Wenzel claimed he received fifty-three boxes of candy for Christmas, but the newspaper said this was a lie and that he received only one—from his sister, Rose Pech.

An experiment was conducted on January 23, 1906, by Dr. John Golden, second assistant to Dr. John Benjamin Murphy of Chicago. Along with witnesses Krugmeier, Conlon, Dr. Nolan, Ryan and Eimmerman, Murphy burned a human corpse comparable to Michael McCarthy's body on the McCarthy property in the open air, in order to test for the time it would take to destroy such a body. The cadaver was of a man who had died of peritonitis, and his body was not embalmed or packed in ice, to ensure the maximum natural state. Using wood from a maple tree, the corpse was destroyed in four and a half hours. The fire was six feet by five feet square and three feet high. No odor was noticeable at a distance of twenty feet, and the remains were small enough to fit inside a cigar box. The odor diminished quickly once the bodily fluids were burned. The smaller bones were ironically

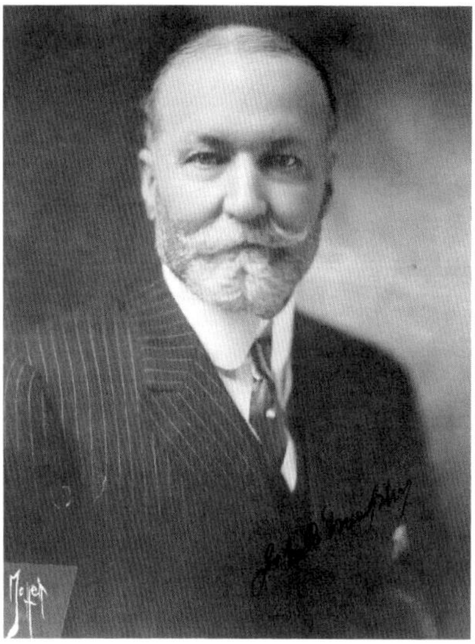

Dr. John Murphy of Appleton, known as "the surgical genius of our generation." *Author's collection.*

preserved longer, because they fell into ashes, where they were protected—the larger bones were subjected to heat and live coals for much longer.

Dr. Murphy, though known as a Chicago doctor, had actually been born in a log cabin in Appleton and educated at Appleton schools. He was present during the infamous 1886 Haymarket Square bombing in Chicago and later attended Theodore Roosevelt following an assassination attempt in Milwaukee. No less an authority than Mayo Clinic cofounder William James Mayo called him "the surgical genius of our generation."

Kabat was a popular target of newspaper editorializing and jailhouse gossip. A day or two before January 27, 1906, the *Neenah Times* editorialized that, "whether guilty or not," Wenzel Kabat was "certainly a degenerate." He "repulsed" even his own mother and was "a scamp on general principles." The *Sun* reported on February 1 that Kabat's physician said he had the "white scourge" of consumption and incorrectly predicted he would not live more than two or three years at the most. Furthermore, Kabat allegedly began "committing slow suicide" by eating soap, but the physician said he saw no evidence of this.

Around February 17, Kabat lost his last friend in the jail, a large brown cat. He would play with the cat on his shoulder, sometimes for several hours a day, "as though it was a child." How a cat got into the jail or where it went is unknown. (The cat allegedly returned months later but could not find Kabat and "left in disgust" that same afternoon.) On February 24, 1906, the *Appleton Crescent* said that Kabat had on more than one occasion threatened to kill Sheriff Koch for depriving him of "some little liberty which was given to other prisoners."

Kabat was transported to Oshkosh on March 17 aboard the 7:52 a.m. train. He was accompanied by Sheriff Koch and Deputy Sheriff Thomas Mitchell. Kabat was handcuffed to Mitchell, and the latter said, "Kabat was very sensitive during the trip to Oshkosh about being handcuffed, and he kept his hand in my pocket so that people would not notice the handcuff."

When they reached the Oshkosh jail, Kabat was so well dressed that the Oshkosh jailer actually mistook him for Mitchell and tried to have the deputy sheriff locked up.

The departure of Kabat now left two prisoners in Appleton: Kaufmann, a young man from Shiocton who had stolen a large quantity of hides in his hometown; and Herman Carl Hafemeister, who was serving thirty days for assaulting his wife, Christina. These two prisoners were put to work building the new jail with contractor Nick Gmeiner, saving the county some expense. Three cells were left intact from the current jail to house these men and one more, should it be needed. Already on March 17, the crew was hard at work, disconnecting steam and water pipes and tearing down telephone wires.

Gmeiner visited Kabat in Oshkosh in early April and reported that Kabat had become gravely ill, despite the earlier claim that Oshkosh was a more healthful jail than Appleton. The papers reported that "Kabat has been under a physician's care a great deal of the time."

Kabat almost escaped from the Oshkosh jail in May. He had secured a drill from two workmen and drilled at the bars of his cell. He also acquired a file under the pretext that he wanted to improve the quality of a deck of playing cards that he had earlier created himself. He was successful in removing two bars and could get into the corridor but got no farther. He next decided to hit his jailer on the head on the evening of Sunday, June 3. Typically, Deputy Sheriff George Adolph Sarau would bring him his food, but on this evening, both Sarau and Sheriff Eber Lane Simpson appeared, and Kabat did not feel confident enough to fight off both men. Later, three saws were found in a magazine underneath his bunk.

On Tuesday, June 5, 1906, Kabat was brought from Oshkosh to Appleton by Sheriff Koch. Once in Appleton, he was placed in a wing of the old building, where he was especially carefully guarded. That afternoon at two o'clock, the court began drawing the jury from a pool of 136 people. By three o'clock, the jury was reduced to 11 people, with the state having two strikes and the defendant eight strikes. Judge Goodland ordered Sheriff Koch to find 40 more potential jurors by two o'clock Wednesday.

The pool on Wednesday consisted of 156 men, and within an hour the jury of 12 was secured. The jury members were as follows: capitalist William Siebert of Seymour; H. Lehrman of Liberty; A. Dexter of Liberty; R.L. Davidson of Liberty; farmer Christ Schroeder of Center; farmer Henry Drephal of Cicero; farmer William Gough of Maple Creek; Leonard H. Hurlburt of Maine; hotel proprietor Anton Koehne of Appleton; H. Jones of Shiocton; farmer George Brown of Ellington; and Rudolph Kirchner of Ellington. For those interested in scanning the complete pool to find the name of a relative, please consult the appendix.

The jury members were brought to Kaukauna by interurban car that same afternoon and were shown McCarthy's farm and other places of interest that would come up during the trial. A.M. Spencer of Appleton and Earl P. Finch of Oshkosh were appointed to the defense, while District Attorney Krugmeier was assisted by Thomas H. Ryan for the state.

Finch had previously been a part of the defense in the infamous 1898 Oshkosh Woodworkers Strike involving the Paine Lumber Company. With him on the defense team were Harry I. Weed, another Oshkosh attorney, and the legendary Clarence Darrow of Chicago. That trial occupied about three weeks and resulted in an acquittal of the defendants on November 2, 1898. The strike is memorialized today at the Oshkosh Public Museum.

Testimony began on Thursday morning, June 7, with Michael's maternal cousin John Sullivan, who lived one and a half miles north of the McCarthy farm. Sullivan testified that Michael "always lived an exemplary life" and seemed "jovial" on the day of his disappearance. Sullivan further said that while it was not unusual for Michael to go on trips, he would often write to Sullivan when he did. Next up was George McCabe, who lived three miles north of the McCarthy farm. He was to tell of Michael's general habits and said that two or three years prior, Michael had "a widow with five children living with him in his house." He further said that Michael was "a trifle peculiar."

Following them was Charles McCarthy, Michael's father. He was followed by Julius Heimke, the farmhand, who was questioned well into the afternoon. Both retold information that we are now well acquainted with.

At one point, John Driscoli testified, merely stating how he had assisted in searching the farm and had found "a large number of nails in the earth and ashes buried under sod." Dr. George Amos Dorsey, head of the anthropology department at the Field Museum, Chicago, testified that the bones found were human and of an adult male and had been recently exposed to intense heat. Dorsey was considered an expert witness, his expertise being comparative anatomy. Dorsey had previously testified during the trial of "sausage king of Chicago" Adolph Luetgert, who had been accused of dismembering his wife and was widely believed to have disposed of her body in his sausage grinder.

In court on Monday, June 11, Kabat was seen shifting his feet, biting his fingernails and clenching his hands. That night, he was unable to sleep. Guards Peter Desotell and Frank Karweich reported that he would cry and groan in his sleep, waking himself up on multiple occasions. The jury was out only ninety-two minutes when it returned with a verdict of guilty of murder in the first degree. Allegedly, one of the jurors (not named) offered an acquittal vote during their informal voting as a joke, but the jury was unanimously in favor of guilty on the formal vote.

The next morning, when asked by the press about the verdict, Kabat said, "Well, I suppose that young Heimke and the two Merritts are satisfied now that I am doomed to the pen. All I feel sorry for in the whole case is for my mother."

Indeed, it appeared that his mother took the verdict hard. On Thursday, June 14, at 2:30 p.m., Mrs. Kabat entered Fred W. and Rudolph H. Radtke's shoe store at 901 College Avenue and asked for a "kaneef." Fred Radtke did not understand her and gave her some shoe buttons. She handed those back and again said "kaneef, kaneef." Radtke now understood and took out a sharp repair knife. She asked that it be wrapped up so she could take it with her, but since she was recognized by Radtke, he refused and contacted the sheriff. This caused Mrs. Kabat to be more closely watched when around her son.

The defense presented a motion to Judge John Goodland on Saturday, June 16, at 10:00 a.m. to have a new trial. Attorney Finch offered six reasons: because justice had not been done; because the verdict was contrary to the evidence; because the verdict was contrary to law; because the court erred in ruling out certain evidence; because the court erred in overruling the defendant's challenges of certain jurors; and because the court erred in the defendant's challenge to the array of jurors.

This motion was rejected, with Goodland declaring, "A more heinous crime cannot be found in the history of criminality." He further called Kabat "a danger to the community." Kabat was further ordered to spend each January 1 in solitary confinement. Kabat's mother wept uncontrollably, and although she did not understand English, she clearly gathered the general intent of Goodland's speech. Kabat was ushered out of the courtroom and back to his jail cell, with his mother and others following him. When he was locked up, his mother sat in a chair, wept more and spoke with her son. A representative of the *Appleton Post* was the first to speak, saying, "Goodbye Kabat. I hope you'll be a better boy in the future than you appear to have been in the past."

Kabat replied, sincerely, "I'll try."

Shortly thereafter, Undersheriff Mitchell handcuffed himself to Kabat and took him to the Northwestern Depot. Kabat was sent to Waupun on the 12:30 p.m. train, accompanied by Mitchell and Officer Bloomer, where he was made convict no. 9684 and assigned to make vests in the tailoring department. Not long after reaching the prison, Wenzel's mother was killed in an unfortunate railroad accident.

On Saturday, August 11, George Altmeyer, a guard at the Outagamie County jail, visited Kabat in Waupun. Altmeyer claimed that Kabat had confessed and he was having the confession copyrighted. The *Kaukauna Sun* doubted this. The *Appleton Post* later published a confession allegedly told to a prisoner at the Oshkosh jail by Kabat while he was there. He confessed to killing not only McCarthy but also a man in Chicago and another in Texas. The *Kaukauna Sun* again doubted the claim, saying it was "preposterous" that "a close-mouthed criminal" like Kabat would talk, and it "put no stock in the report." The one report the *Kaukauna Sun* did believe was that "Wenzel Kabat is a model prisoner at the state penitentiary and is 'trusty' in the tailoring department." This tailoring skill would come in handy later.

The court of Brown County made a judgment around September 27, 1906, that those who bought cattle from Kabat would have to pay a second time—now to the estate of Michael McCarthy. Those ordered to pay again included farmer Andrew Keating, who had purchased some calves, as well as Robert Ehnerd of Wrightstown. The latter did not accept the court's decision and filed suit. Around December 13, 1906, the McCarthy estate and Ehnerd settled the suit out of court concerning cattle Ehnerd had purchased from Wenzel Kabat for several hundred dollars. The positions were clear: the McCarthys felt they were robbed of property, while Ehnerd had little desire to pay for property that he had already paid for once. The *Kaukauna Sun* editorialized as follows: "Things would be in a pretty condition in this country if any thief or murderer could forge a bill of sale, take the life of the owner or send him away, and then sell the property to those who should know better than buy questionable holdings." Whether Keating or Ehnerd really knew better is not known, but certainly it must have been suspicious to buy cattle from a stranger at such a discount.

On Friday morning, December 21, 1906, Timothy McCarthy (Michael's younger brother) was given a preliminary examination in the justice court at Wrightstown. He was charged with intent to kill Frank Ehnerd, the Wrightstown butcher who had purchased cattle from Wenzel Kabat. He was bound over in the sum of $1,000 to appear in the municipal court at Green Bay on Thursday, January 3, 1907. The *Kaukauna Sun* speculated that McCarthy might be sent to "an asylum" because he was "a nervous wreck." Amazingly, this story appears to have never been followed up by the newspapers; we do not know what became of Timothy in the courts, though he ultimately moved to Denver.

On March 6, 1907, a hearing on descent in the estate of Katherine Sullivan McCarthy, the deceased mother of Michael McCarthy, was held in county court. Although Katherine had been dead for more than ten years, her holdings were now unexpectedly messed up. The woman had previously given the McCarthy homestead in the town of Kaukauna to her sons equally, all of whom quitclaimed their shares to Michael McCarthy. In view of the demise of Michael McCarthy, it was necessary that a judgment determining the descent of the property should be entered of record and filed in county court so that his property could be properly disposed of according to the will made by the murdered man. Henry Gloudemans, who was currently the property caretaker, apparently did not stay on the McCarthy farm long. Charles McCarthy, through Michael's estate, sold the farm to Martin VanZeeland on February 25, 1909, for $10,800. Charles himself left the state, relocating to Mankato, Kansas.

A very bizarre story came to light on June 28, 1909, and indirectly involved our villain. Though dead, a former Appleton man named Garrow, mixed up with Wenzel Kabat in a lawsuit shortly before the latter killed McCarthy, had helped the police of Manitowoc and Sterling, Colorado, clear up the mystery of Edward Huebner of Manitowoc, who was given up for lost or dead because no letters had been received from him for a long time. Garrow's body had been found in Sterling several weeks earlier, lifeless by his own hand or through murder. On the body were found several letters addressed to Huebner, and it was the theory of the police that the former Appletonian had intercepted the letters sent from Manitowoc to Huebner in the west. It was considered possible that a photograph of the dead man would be sent to the penitentiary so that Kabat could say whether or not it was that of Garrow.

The Further Tale of Julius Heimke

Many in Kaukauna suspected that Julius Heimke knew more than he let on and had helped convict Kabat in part to get blame removed from himself as an accomplice. Shortly after the trial ended, Heimke left the Fox Cities and made his way to Dayton, Ohio, where he worked until returning in March 1908. Within a month of his return to Kaukauna, Heimke and one Will

Burhans were implicated in the robbery of the train depot, using a poker to pry open the cashbox and steal fifty-seven dollars. Night operator Ernest Rowe had stepped away to run an errand at Charles Ristau's hotel when the pair swooped in. They might have gotten away with it if Burhans had not started spending the loot lavishly at a south-side tavern. He was picked up on a train to Antigo, and Heimke confessed as soon as Burhans was collared.

Although mathematicians Merrill Flood and Melvin Dresher wouldn't introduce "the prisoners' dilemma" for decades, Heimke and Burhans found themselves in a real-world version of the classic brain-teaser. By May, Burhans considered pleading guilty, but he realized that if he did so, Heimke could plead not guilty and place all the blame on him. This would result in Burhans potentially serving a heavy sentence and Heimke going free. Instead, they ultimately pled guilty together, and Judge Goodland sentenced them both to one year in the reformatory, much less than the twenty-year maximum. Goodland advised the young men to quit drinking.

Due to good behavior, Heimke was out after only eleven months. He quickly returned to his petty crimes. In March 1911, while living in an apartment above the Ressman and Bahcall dry-cleaning establishment in Appleton, he wandered downstairs and stole a measly $4.20 in cash. Heimke was again brought before Judge Goodland, who again sentenced him to one year. This time, he was sent to Waupun rather than the reformatory. The newspapers speculated that Heimke and Kabat would now be able to see each other again, though we have no evidence that they did.

Heimke's imprisonment became an ordeal for his whole family. His wife, Ellen, moved to Waupun to be closer to him and took up employment at the Beaumont Hotel as a maid. She was soon arrested for stealing clothes from a guest and ended up in prison herself. Her sentence was only thirty days, but it was not in Waupun—she was sent to the women's prison in Taycheedah, just outside of Fond du Lac.

In early October 1911, Heimke wrote to a prominent College Avenue businessman from Waupun State Prison, asking for his assistance in securing parole. He said he had "turned over a new leaf" and wanted to support his "girl wife" who would "be only half cared for" that coming winter. He wanted to work as a driver for a livery barn or on a grocery wagon, as he believed this was the kind of work he would like. He did not succeed in achieving parole but seems to have escaped his life of crime after being released from Waupun.

KABAT ON THE LOOSE

Around September 1914, Kabat began telling a prison official that he was going to escape. The official is not named, but he was an Irishman, and Kabat called him "mean" and "a real 'flannel-mouth'" (someone who speaks in an unclear, muffled or sluggish manner). His boast soon proved true; Kabat escaped from Waupun on October 3, 1914. Kabat later said he escaped prison by sawing through the bars with a saw he found in the prison workshop, opened a door with a key he had fashioned from a piece of hickory and then scaled the walls and went to an automobile that was waiting outside. While in the halls, he entered the tailor shop and took a suit of civilian clothes. The *Appleton Crescent* alleged that he escaped with the help of jewelers' files "that had been smuggled to him in some manner." The automobile may have been furnished by an unnamed man whose prison term had expired one day before, according to the warden, Reverend Daniel Woodward. Or, perhaps more likely, there never was an automobile. Later versions of the story omit this part entirely.

Once over the wall, Kabat hid in the shadows as a couple walked by. An off-duty prison guard even spotted him, to whom Kabat said, "Hello." The guard, not recognizing Kabat, said, "Hello" back and continued walking. Kabat went to a friend's house and sat on his porch, applying a sweet-scented liquid used for brushing teeth on his shoes. He figured that, this way, the bloodhounds would think his friend was harboring him and be thrown off the trail. He next left town and slept in a schoolhouse. Upon waking, he went to Green Lake and then Portage before joining up with some boys who helped him flee the state—he did not cross the border for two weeks.

Upon his escape, Kabat assumed the name of the deputy warden at Waupun. Kabat later claimed he began a search for Michael McCarthy, who he said was still alive. He allegedly searched Mexico, South America and throughout the United States. This was certainly false. On Wednesday, November 10, 1915, the board of supervisors of Outagamie County adopted a resolution offering a reward of $1,000 for the capture of Wenzel Kabat. A committee consisting of supervisors Lueck, Ryan and Ferdinand D. Zocholl was appointed to act with the district attorney in this matter.

Kabat settled in Austin, Minnesota, in 1915 and became employed at a packing plant, at one point being a foreman with seventy-two men under him. Today, Austin is best known as the birthplace of Spam. As William Coles (sometimes written Kohls), Kabat was twice nominated to be a candidate for the Minnesota State Legislature. He was a personal friend of the police chief and the sheriff in Austin. He moved to Ellsworth, Minnesota, and set up a successful tailoring establishment. He worked this job for a time and then sold the business "to a Jew" for a profit and returned to Austin, taking up residence at 909 East Bridge Street.

Around January 21, 1917, the son of the owner of the packing plant was looking at an old pamphlet called "Men Wanted" in *Ludwig's Detective Bulletin* and recognized Coles as Kabat. The prison had received a tip from one of their convicts that Kabat could be found along the "main line" in Minnesota, so they had sent photos in that direction.

When Sheriff Nick Nicholsen entered Kabat's home tailoring shop, the Austin Steam Laundry, on Tuesday, January 23, he said, "Say Coles, they want you in Wisconsin."

Kabat replied with a laugh, "I guess not."

The sheriff showed him the photo and asked, "Well, whose photo is this?"

Kabat was caught and said, "That's me, I guess. I have a skirt here which I promised that I would have ready tonight for the lady. I have not finished cleaning it. Will you permit me to do so?" They allowed this, and when he was done, Kabat put on his coat. "Well, I'm ready now." He was then taken to jail.

The local newspaper had been quite fooled by Kabat, calling him "a respected business man" with "a two year record of thorough integrity." When he was captured and admitted he was the right man, they swallowed his claim of innocence—Kabat claimed that the McCarthy house had burned down and bones were found inside, making him a suspect without any real evidence. We know, of course, this was not the reality. Interestingly, the papers also pointed out an odd coincidence—Michael McCarthy allegedly was the stepbrother of a man named Michael Harrington, who operated a hotel in Austin.

The sheriff in Austin who took Kabat into custody was awarded only $100, as the Wisconsin attorney general declared the $1,000 offered by Outagamie County invalid. The sheriff planned to share the money with the boy who saw Kabat's picture. An interesting juxtaposition took place as Kabat boarded the train back to Wisconsin. A marching band was playing an exuberant tune, which many mistook to be a farewell to their friend Coles. In fact, it just so happened that Kabat was leaving at the same moment that Company G was returning home from the Mexican border.

On Thursday, January 25, 1917, Kabat arrived at the Waupun prison at 7:30 p.m. and was given a red suit—the color of escapees. The *Manitowoc*

Herald reported in June 1917 that Kabat was "completely paralyzed on one side of his body and prison physicians say that he has but a short time to live." They received the information from a Waupun man who was a delegate of the Knights of Pythias and a personal friend of the warden at Waupun. Kabat was reported to be aware that he was near death, and the prison allowed him "greater liberty and more privileges" than he had prior to escaping.

Although only the prison guards know for sure, the next two decades seem to have been unremarkable. On January 2, 1941, Kabat was pardoned by Republican governor Julius P. Heil over the decision of the pardon board to deny his request. Attorney Mark Catlin Jr. petitioned on his behalf, while Albert Krugmeier (the original prosecutor) argued that Kabat never expressed remorse and that there were no extenuating circumstances that would forgive him for such a heinous act. He also suspected that Kabat was being "crafty," because each time he applied for parole over his many years, he "coincidentally" hired an attorney who was of the same political party as the sitting governor. Even the state psychiatrist, Winnebago Central State Hospital for the Insane superintendent Dr. Peter Bell, said he could find nothing in the man's record that would suggest leniency was appropriate, referring to Kabat as "mentally deranged" and "sexually promiscuous."

Heil issued a message:

> *I am today pardoning Wenzel E. Kabat, who was sentenced to life imprisonment and committed to state prison at Waupun on June 15, 1906. Mr. Kabat is now and has been for a number of years eligible for parole. The parole authorities are willing to parole him. I am pardoning Mr. Kabat because I too believe that he is now ready and able to be a good, law-abiding upright member of society. Mr. Kabat's record of work and industry in responsible prison positions over the last 34 years and his general good conduct in prison have substantially helped merit the consideration I have given him. Arrangements have been made to aid Mr. Kabat in stabilizing and adjusting himself in private life to which he is returning. Mr. Kabat's representatives and the persons in closest contact with him at prison believe he is ready and able to take his place in society. I am accepting this belief.*

A few days after his release, on a Thursday afternoon, the white-haired Kabat returned to Appleton with Mark Catlin Jr. wearing his prison-issued gray suit of clothes, overcoat and cap. He visited with Mark Catlin Sr. and met Thomas Ryan Jr.—the son of Thomas H. Ryan, the prosecutor in

1906 who had since become a judge. Kabat told the younger Ryan that he had no ill will toward his father, and if he had, he would have "pulled his whiskers" in 1914 when he escaped. While there, a fire truck went by with sirens blaring, making Kabat nervous. "That's a fire," Catlin Sr. explained.

"Oh, that's the way they do it now. I thought it was the police after me," Kabat laughed.

Newly released, Kabat figured he would take up tailoring, as this was his most practiced trade. Though the Depression was hardly over, Kabat did not worry. "There isn't any depression for a man with an imagination," he said. "A man can always go into business for himself and make it go."

Epilogue

In the 1930s, Dan McCarthy, Michael McCarthy's nephew, was a lawyer and at one time was a Kansas state senator. He married Katherine O'Loughlin, one of the first women from Kansas to serve in Congress. She served during President Franklin D. Roosevelt's first term.

Wenzel Kabat ended up leaving the state for a while but eventually returned and took up residence at the McCormick home in Green Bay

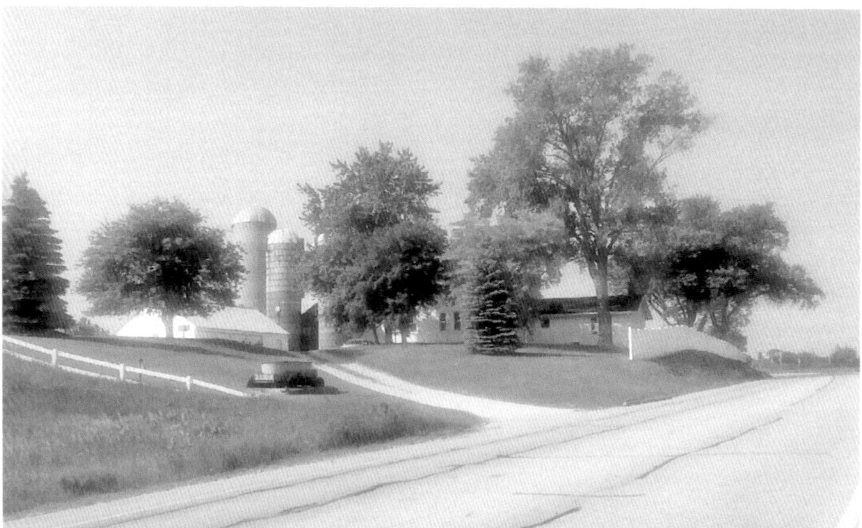

The Michael McCarthy house as it stood in 2017, surrounded by a subdivision. *Author's collection.*

from December 14, 1961, to January 11, 1962. He would later live at 215½ Pine Street in Green Bay. He passed away on March 20, 1966, without any fanfare. No obituary or news story was published reminding the community of Kabat's deeds. He was buried at the St. Phillip Catholic Church in Green Bay, with Reverend Monsignor Theodore Verbeten officiating.

The "cursed" land was sold a handful of times. In January 1946, Martin VanZeeland sold the McCarthy farm to his son Norbert. The farm was kept in the VanZeeland family for many more years, being sold again from the estate of Norbert to his son Terry on February 1, 1974. Terry VanZeeland passed away in October 2010, and the land was sold to the Collins family, with whom the property remains at the time of this writing. Interestingly, a wealthy subdivision has been built up around the farm, but the original McCarthy homestead has been left untouched.

6

THE BOO GANG

Readers who enjoyed the story of Wenzel Kabat may have wondered halfway through: who was "Sleepy Tom" Cahill, and what was the Boo Gang? Chances are, even if you grew up in Appleton, you never heard of this band of miscreants.

The origins remain unclear and may have been lost to time. We know that this so-called gang was based in Appleton's Third Ward, around St. Mary's Catholic Church, and was primarily made up of young men engaged in petty crimes. These were not high-profile bank robbers or murderers. Only a few of their names and crimes remain on record today.

In April 1901, several gang members were "rushing the growler," and two, identified as "Hickey" and "Tracy," were arrested. One was found in a woodshed and the other was under a haystack with his feet sticking out. This Hickey was almost certainly a member of the Hickey family who lived at 527–531 West Sixth Street. The "growler" in this context may refer to a horse-drawn police carriage, with the boys attempting to free a fellow troublemaker.

In June 1901, the Boo Gang developed an "organized system" of chicken stealing. They were said to enjoy midnight meetings of chicken stew, rye bread and beer, at least until one of them was caught raiding Martin Walter's henhouse at 505 Walnut Street.

In February 1902, the Boo Gang was said to be raising money from acquaintances to bail two of their members out of the county workhouse where they were breaking rocks. The amount needed was fifty dollars.

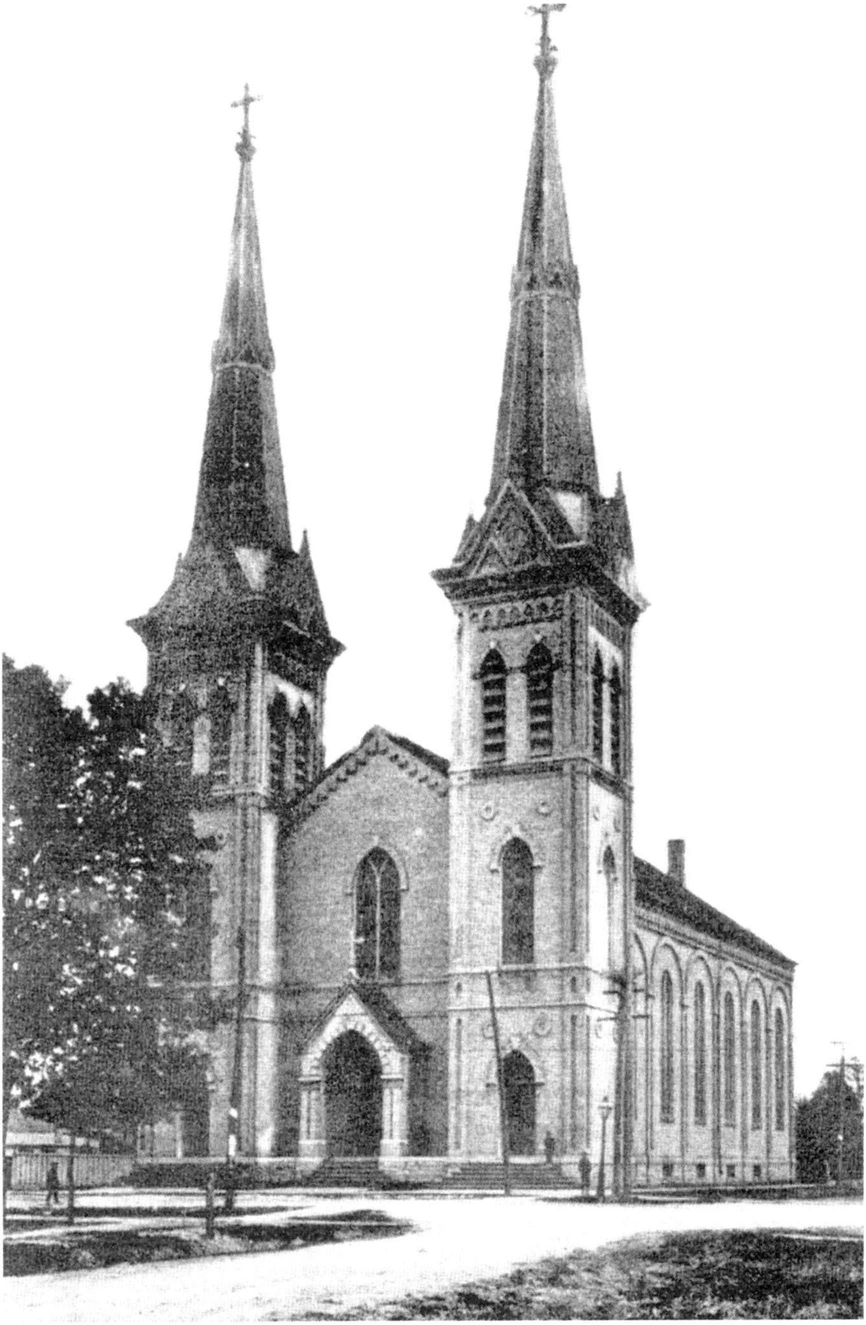

St. Mary's Catholic Church, the centerpiece in the neighborhood haunted by the Boo Gang. *Appleton Public Library*.

In April 1903, Daniel Hannigan, identified as an "aged man," accused a group of "young toughs" of bringing him to a saloon and then stealing forty dollars from him. The police vowed to raid the known hangouts of the Boo Gang.

In November 1905, "Sleepy Tom" Cahill was held on the charge of burglary, as mentioned in the last chapter.

"Sleepy Tom" Cahill was said to be one of the few surviving members of the gang. In July 1907, Cahill, along with Bert Saeger, entered the store of Peter Gabe and stole six razors. After his arrest, he was to choose between a thirty-dollar fine and thirty days' hard labor at the county workhouse. Saeger and Cahill were also suspected of being involved in a post office robbery at Embarrass.

7

THE KIDNAPPING OF FRANCES WEBB

Kidnapping is a rare crime, but it is one of the most traumatic for a family to endure. The practice achieved widespread attention in the 1930s, with the kidnapping of Charles Lindbergh's child, as well as two prominent brewers from Minneapolis, Edward Bremer and William Hamm. Many have credited the Lindbergh case with prodding Congress into passing a federal law against kidnapping, though a closer examination of the timeline suggests it was already in the process of passing such a bill.

Though kidnapping came into vogue in the early twentieth century, the "snatch racket" is a timeless crime. Some of our earliest myths and legends tell of the practice—think of the Trojan War, sparked by the kidnapping of Helen. Even Julius Caesar was not immune, having been kidnapped by pirates. One of the most notorious crimes in Neenah was a kidnapping that took place in the years before the federal law came to pass. It is here that our tale begins.

Six-year-old Frances B. Webb, daughter of James Webb, left her house at 122 First Street on the morning of Tuesday, April 13, 1926, to walk the one block to Roosevelt School. Despite the short distance, she never made it. By midafternoon, her parents and friends were searching the roads of Winnebago County for any sign of her and offered a $500 reward for anyone who could help. Her description was released to the public: that morning, she was dressed in a green fur coat, stocking cap, scarf, high brown boots and tan stockings. Classmates told police they saw a tall, dark-complexioned man lure Frances into a Chevrolet coupe near the school.

While any abduction would have shocked the community, this one particularly caught everyone's attention: James Webb was the president of Krueger Hardware, and his wife, Laura, was the daughter of Maurice Edward Barnett. Barnett was the proprietor of the city's leading pharmacy, and Maurice's father-in-law had been William Krueger, the hardware firm's patriarch. These were prominent and wealthy business families in Neenah. A note soon arrived demanding $3,000 for the girl.

There is no way to properly describe the panic and fear that gripped Neenah. Still a small community today, the city was ever so much smaller in the 1920s. There was no one who did not know the Barnett or Krueger families personally, and they spent the day worrying, fearing that an innocent child was dead…or worse. Maurice Barnett may have been particularly concerned. His only son, Maurice Jr., had been killed during the Meuse-Argonne Offensive in 1918, putting an end to the Barnett name. How much pain would it add to lose not only a brave son but also a cherished granddaughter?

The panic, luckily, subsided before the next newspaper update hit the doorstep. As quickly as the excitement started, relief came to Neenah, and the ransom had not been paid. Twelve hours after her disappearance,

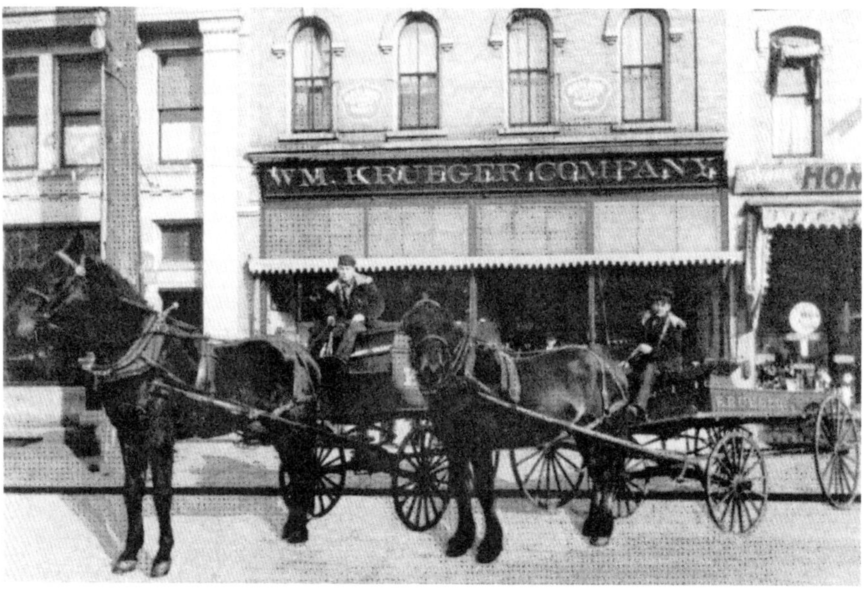

The Krueger Hardware Company, which still exists more than 150 years later in Neenah. *Neenah Historical Society.*

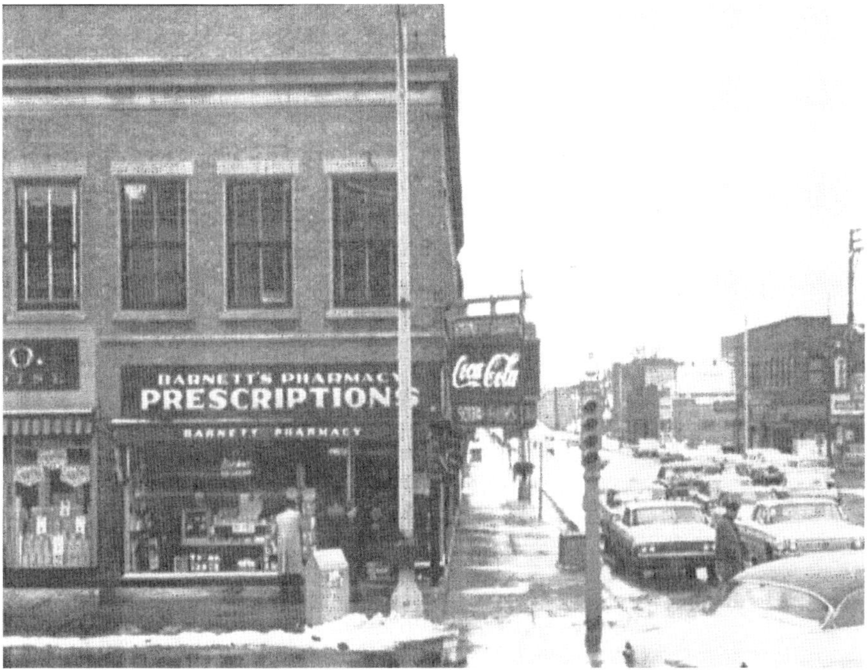

Barnett's Pharmacy, a successful business in Neenah's downtown. *Neenah Historical Society.*

Frances showed up at the John (or James) Mann farm in St. Peter, in western Fond du Lac County, on "the Sheboygan road." Her abductor had dropped her off there, instructing the farmer that he would return the next day. Mann wanted no part in the matter and immediately called the authorities at Fond du Lac.

But who was the kidnapper? On Sunday, April 18, the culprit was revealed to be Frederick W. Runde, twenty-six, of Neenah. Police arrested Runde on his way to meet New London coed Beatrice O. Monsted, twenty, in Madison. He was identified by Carl F. Krueger, a former Neenah resident and relative of the Krueger family, who just happened to be in the capital and recognized the wanted man. In fact, at one point, the two had been neighbors. Runde was the son of Otto G. Runde, a German immigrant who passed in 1917, and his wife, Mary. Frederick's upbringing was a bit chaotic. His parents divorced and remarried each other while he was a child, and his mother ran a boardinghouse on Oak Street, with strangers constantly coming and going. Frederick left home immediately following his father's passing, enlisting in the U.S. Navy during World War I. While away, his

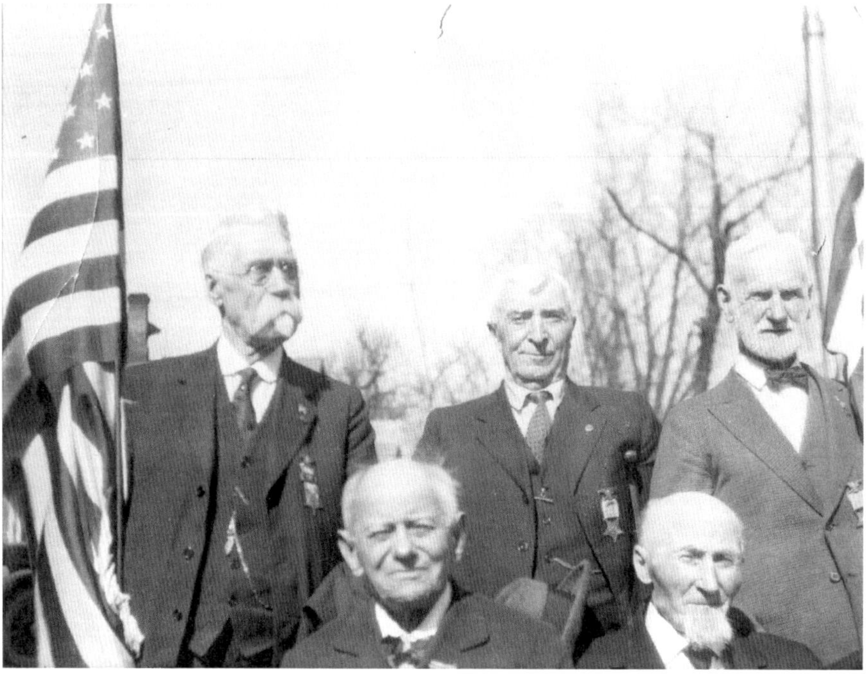

Thad Sheerin (*middle, back row*), the last Civil War soldier in Neenah. *Neenah Historical Society*.

mother married Thaddeus Sheerin, notable for being Neenah's last living Civil War veteran.

Monsted was the daughter of Dr. John Winfield Monsted, a celebrated physician in New London who was also the county coroner and a stockholder in the First National Bank. Police Chief Charles Henry Watts and two Pinkerton detectives grilled Runde all evening but were unable to get a confession from him. Regardless, they determined that his handwriting matched that of the ransom note and learned that he had formerly been employed by Mr. Webb, which would explain how he knew who Frances was.

Runde was brought to Oshkosh on Monday, but his case was continued until April 27 in order to allow for a mental exam. Attorney John Frederick Kluwin was assigned to represent Runde. Kluwin was a prominent member of the community in Oshkosh, having served for a while as city attorney. In 1911, he took over the management of the Oshkosh Indians baseball team and led them to the league pennant.

Police were quickly piecing the story together: Runde had stolen a car in Fond du Lac, where he was living at the Retlaw Hotel under an assumed name. On his way to visit his mother in Neenah, he consumed a pint of gin and became intoxicated. He abducted the girl in Neenah, less than two blocks from his mother's house, without much thought as to the reason why; Runde and the girl had known each other and had been friendly for the girl's entire life. Her father was a target merely on impulse. Runde and Mr. Webb had only ever had one negative encounter: Runde damaged a company truck while delivering a load of furniture to an attorney named Erling K. Loverud in Stoughton. But this had been a fairly minor affair.

Runde had secured pen and paper in Menasha at William Erhardt's Tourist Inn Café on Milwaukee Street, a speakeasy he frequently visited, and mailed the ransom note in Appleton by handing it to a carrier. He then returned to Fond du Lac by driving on Highway 55 down the east side of Lake Winnebago after stopping for a short nap at the side of the road in Sherwood. During the car ride, Runde purchased cookies and candy for the girl. The reason he dropped the girl off at a farm, he claimed, was because, when he sobered up, he realized that his victim knew him and had extensive wealth and influence. The only way to get away with the crime would be to kill Frances, which he had no intention to do, so he fled.

Runde was found to have occasional "dizzy spells" related to his heavy drinking of bathtub gin, but he was not mentally unstable. After doctors declared Runde sane, he pled guilty, and Judge Arthur Hibbard Goss sentenced him to life in Waupun Prison. He went from being a kidnapper to a lifetime convict in a mere two weeks. Runde had expected to get a mere three years, not being aware of how strict the law was; he would have received a far lesser sentence for just about any crime he could have committed. Interestingly, Goss had served as a judge for thirty-one years, and Runde was the first man he ever sentenced to life. Under Wisconsin statutes at the time, life was the minimum penalty for a ransom kidnapping.

Runde tried for a pardon in December 1927 but was denied by Governor Fred R. Zimmerman. The next attempt was more successful; on December 26, 1928, Zimmerman reduced Runde's time from life to fifteen years. Since Runde's conviction, a new law was on the books that offered lesser penalties for kidnappers who don't harm their victims. The new maximum was thirty years, not life. As no harm came to Webb, it seemed only fair to Zimmerman to give Runde this second chance. Runde's attorney noted that his "penalty would have been no greater, under the laws of 1925, had he ravaged this child's body and even killed her to cover up the crime." The record showed that Runde had actually comforted rather than hurt Webb, offering his skeepskin coat when she got cold. Clearly, the punishment did not fit the crime. While behind bars, Runde struck up a friendship with Jule Beard, a prisoner from Canada. Beard passed in early 1931 and left his small fortune—$300 in the commissary—to Runde. Beard is today still in Waupun, buried in the prison cemetery.

With Runde behind bars and Frances growing into an adolescent, life was largely idyllic for the Webb family. But apparently being wealthy and well known in such a small town made them an easy mark, and there was to be at least one more attempt to extort them of their hard-earned money. No doubt the ongoing Depression made some people desperate and resentful.

On the morning of April 22, 1931, James Webb's world was shaken again. Someone had mailed him a letter from the Neenah post office demanding that he throw a package containing $3,000 from the Soo Line train where it meets Highway 26. Police were contacted, and they had M.W. Krueger throw a dummy package off the train at 11:30 p.m. Krueger was Webb's wife's uncle, approximately seventy years old by this time. Around midnight, Greenville farmer Roland David Hassinger, thirty-four, drove up and retrieved the package. Police turned on their lights, and Hassinger started running. The police opened fire, riddling the car with bullets. Hassinger was arrested. He denied knowing Webb or sending the letter, saying he was in Milwaukee at the time. He just happened to see a package and stopped to look. Hassinger was held overnight while the police could confirm his alibi.

Behind the scenes, a letter-writing campaign was begun in Neenah by some prominent businessmen to get Runde pardoned. Neenah Paper Company's first vice-president, Daniel Kevill Brown, wrote to say that Runde "has already paid a sufficient penalty for what to myself and others looked more like a foolish prank or a youngster's idea of revenge rather than a really criminal motive." Gilbert Paper Company vice-president Frank J. Schneller expressed similar confidence. He noted that he had been in correspondence with Runde and had in the past hired Waupun parolees with great success. Schneller essentially told the governor that if a parole was granted, Runde could be hired on at Gilbert Paper.

A petition was also circulating around Neenah that eventually secured the signatures of 122 businessmen and other notable citizens who felt that Runde deserved clemency. Employees of Jandrey's Department Store, almost exclusively women, also asked for Runde to be released. The names "Webb" and "Krueger" were not on the list, other than Walter A. Krueger, not believed to be a relative.

Prosecutor D.K. Allen was less than convinced. He wrote the governor to stress that Runde "was involved in more matters of a criminal or questionable nature than almost anybody I know of." This is clearly hyperbole, but Allen had no intention of letting the state go light on a kidnapper. And the accusation was not without foundation. Runde's record showed that he had passed worthless checks "five or six times" in Appleton and had once stolen a car in Neenah other than the one he stole on the day of the kidnapping. There was also an incident in which Runde threatened his uncle, A.W. Anderson, that he would kill himself if Anderson did not bring him $1,000.

Perhaps the greatest letters in Runde's favor came from within the prison. The warden personally recommended parole, noting the superior record of the man and again insisting the child was never harmed and that Runde had served in the military with distinction during World War I. A deputy related a story about how an inmate named Norton tried to kill him (the deputy), and Runde came to the guard's aid. After the fight was stopped, Norton turned to Runde and said, "If I ever meet you on the outside, I'll kill you, you son of a bitch." Having chosen law and order over allowing a murder to happen was about the finest act of redemption anyone could ask. On other occasions, Runde had intercepted letters written in invisible ink and once found a gun that had been mailed into the prison. Runde's occupation while in Waupun was prison photographer, taking the mug shots of his fellow inmates.

The prosecution countered the warden's claims of Runde's serving with distinction in the military. In a letter to the governor, it was pointed out that Runde served on the USS *Carola* and likely only saw eleven days of battle in France. In what might be considered a low blow, Runde was compared with Maurice Barnett, Frances Webb's uncle, who was killed in France. The implication was clear: the Webb family had made the greater sacrifices than Runde on repeated occasions. The letter also pointed out that Laura Webb had been "seriously ill" and in the hospital because of the kidnapping and still lived "in constant fear of Runde's release."

Runde applied for a pardon yet again in November 1932, this time from Governor Philip F. LaFollette, son of the legendary Robert "Fighting Bob" LaFollette. The request was granted, and Runde immediately set out to start a new life. He moved to the southern suburbs of Milwaukee and, by 1936, was married and had his first of two daughters. Runde lived out the rest of his life without attracting negative publicity and passed on in Milwaukee on January 31, 1981.

Frances Webb seems to have been unfazed by her ordeal. She grew up and married Robert Willard Ozanne in June 1940, the son of a doctor and himself a professor of history specializing in the Wisconsin labor movement. They lived a comfortable life in Madison, raising three sons. One grandson, Ismael Ozanne, went on to achieve a certain degree of fame as the district attorney for Dane County (Madison), a position he holds at the time of this writing.

8

A HOT TIME AT THE BLAZING STUMP

At this point, readers will realize that brothels and houses of ill repute were not uncommon in the Fox Cities. But one remains legendary above all others, even close to a century later: the Blazing Stump of Darboy, said to be run by an elusive "Ma Gooley" (of whom no record apparently exists). Though the building would change its name over the years, the newspapers insisted on referring to that den of sin as the Blazing Stump, a name it could never shake. This chapter will be a brief attempt to chronicle the history of the Blazing Stump roadhouse in southeast Appleton. Although most records (such as arrest reports) have long since been destroyed, some fragments remain thanks to diligent news reporting.

The Flynn-DeBrue-Wichmann Years

Possibly the first owner of the Blazing Stump was Agnes Flynn of Chilton, the daughter of Irish immigrants Patrick Flynn and Ellen Gallagher. The building seems to have been erected decades before she came along but had not yet acquired its reputation.

On January 20, 1897, Agnes married Joseph DeBrue of Kaukauna. DeBrue was born in Green Bay to Belgian Americans John DeBrue and Mary DeBreuer. The new couple had five children: Genevieve, Leona, Jerome, Margaret and Arthur. Joseph was a foreman in a machine shop, and the family lived in Kaukauna on Amanda Street, a dead-end drive.

Agnes and Joseph seem to have been divorced between 1910 and 1920, though a record has not yet been found. Joseph died in 1945 and is buried in St. Mary's Cemetery, Kaukauna, along with daughters Genevieve and Leona. Genevieve married Carl Andersen and had a very distinguished life. She had been a partner in the Service Hardware Store until 1964 and was a post office employee from 1922 until her retirement in 1963, as assistant postmaster. She was a member of the Kaukauna Business and Professional Women's Club, the Lady Foresters of Sacred Heart Court, the Catholic Knights, the Red Cross Grey Ladies, the Kaukauna Hospital Auxiliary, St. Mary Altar Society and the Knights of Columbus Ladies.

The newspapers don't say when Agnes purchased the Blazing Stump, but it seems to have been between husbands. There is no indication that Joseph DeBrue had any connection to the place, and she was already the proprietor before husband number two.

The divorced Agnes Flynn, now an empty nester, married Herman C. Wichmann (son of Charles F. Wichmann and Mary Berger) on September 11, 1922 in Menominee, Michigan. Herman was originally from Brandon, a small village near Fond du Lac known for its hemp production. Justice of the Peace Michael J. Buckley performed the service, with Mrs. J. Gillis of Fond du Lac as witness. Interestingly, Herman was approximately twenty years Agnes's junior.

Around September 1924, Agnes Wichmann was able to get a divorce from her second husband, Herman, on the grounds of cruel and inhumane treatment. Along with two other witnesses, Agnes testified that she was repeatedly beaten, had her nose broken twice and was abused with vile language. Agnes was given complete control of the Blazing Stump, with Herman not allowed to interfere.

The divorce was not the end for this couple. Herman Wichmann was arrested on October 10, 1924, in Neenah for assault and battery. He was accused of beating his former wife. He pled guilty and paid a small fine. Around this time, he was also fined twenty-five dollars for carrying a concealed .32 pistol on College Avenue in Appleton.

Amazingly, Agnes and Herman were back in Menominee on November 22, 1924, getting remarried. Justice Buckley was again the officiant, and witnesses were Nellie Buckley (the justice's daughter) and Mrs. George Soakley, both of Menominee. It seems that they sold the Blazing Stump around October or November to one Louis Soffa, who changed the name to the Clover Inn.

On December 7, police raided 1022 Second Avenue in Appleton, the residence of Herman and Agnes Wichmann. They found a woman who said her name was Jennie Miller, a prostitute. City-employed teamster George Cleophas Doine was picked up but swore to police he had no idea he was in a brothel; he was released. He said he saw a "chimney fire" and went inside to throw salt on it. He was told not to go near chimney fires anymore. Exactly how Doine explained the mess to his wife and children is another story. An entire room of the Wichmann residence was found to be converted to a bar, and the liquor was seized (this was during Prohibition). The Wichmanns were both held in jail on $1,000 bond. By the end of the month, they were fined $100 by Judge Albert Spencer, whom you may recall from the tale of Wenzel Kabat.

The Wichmanns, with or without their roadhouse, continued to be trouble. In April 1925, Herman was arrested for assaulting his brother William and for being intoxicated. While in the jail, he accused his wife of being an informant of the "sponge squad" (Prohibition enforcement).

In mid-December 1924, the Clover Inn was hit by two masked robbers. They came in, started shooting and forced employee Ernie Mandie to march a mile down Darboy Road. The men took fifty dollars from the cash register and stole two slot machines believed to have approximately eighty dollars in silver. When the bandits left, Mandie walked to the nearest farmhouse and got together a small posse of farmers with shotguns, but it was too late. When owner Louis Soffa arrived at the inn, he found bullet holes all over the premises. The tragedy became opportunity, and by New Year's, the roadhouse was completely remodeled.

By February 1926, the building again changed hands, this time going from Soffa to A.E. Altizer.

Enter the Milwaukee Mafia

During much of the 1930s, the Blazing Stump successfully stayed out of the newspapers. Whether this means the place was "clean" or just lucky is unclear. But it stumbled in 1939 and had its last hurrah in 1941.

On March 14, 1939, the Calumet County sheriff rounded up six "inmates" (prostitutes), who pled guilty to prostitution and were fined $100 each. They were also ordered to leave the county. Interestingly, the two men who were caught only had to pay fines of $15.

A twenty-year-old woman, whom the newspaper described as "platinum blonde with spectacles," and whom we will call "Trista," testified that she met mobster Nick Machi at the Gay Spot in Milwaukee on April 3, 1941. Machi said he had a job for her that would be "the chance of a lifetime." At 1:30 a.m. on April 5, she was driven to DePere by Machi and Nick Gentile, where they met Jack Forman, the operator of Joy's Lunch. She started "working" on April 8 with two other girls. A few days later, Machi picked her up and brought her to the Riverside Tavern in Sheboygan Falls, and he took $25 from her. The owner of the Riverside gave Machi $50, and when the girl was done on April 30, she gave Machi $57. On April 30, Trista was brought to the Club Royal in Plymouth and in early May was brought to the Blazing Stump in Appleton. Machi received about $115 more from her. On June 1, a woman at the Blazing Stump also gave Machi $100. By June 5, Machi had taken another $70 from the prostitute.

In May 1941, Salvatore Gagliano, Louis Fazio and a man named Duffy set up a fifteen-year-old Milwaukee girl (who lived at a foster home in Wauwatosa) with a brothel called Maxine's (also known as the Colonial Club, owned by Maxine and Chris Constance), two miles west of Sheboygan Falls on County Highway C (across from O'Neill's restaurant). Gagliano, also known as "Teddy Capp, the singing bartender," met the girl on the nights of May 1 and May 2 at Nick du Laveris's tavern (corner of Fourth and Wells), telling her that he had a job for her. After taking her to an eastside hotel (where he falsely told her they would be meeting with friends), they went to a barroom and met up with Fazio and Duffy. The three men drove her to Maxine's. The girl worked there for a while but rebelled when asked to perform for a group of young Sheboygan businessmen. Maxine drove her back to Nick du Laveris's tavern, where the girl paid Gagliano $100 to be "released."

While at a Milwaukee hotel on May 24, Nick Machi and Trista were arrested by the police, and attorney Mario Megna showed up to bail them out. While Machi and Megna had known each other for years, this was the first interaction Megna had with Trista, whom he quickly took under his wing.

Two days later, Nick Machi and Trista were on trial for disorderly conduct, represented by Megna. The case was dismissed; the same day, Megna represented the woman in juvenile court before Judge Walter Schinz, where she was trying to get custody of her illegitimate eighteen-month-old son. Megna instructed his client to say she was a waitress. Outside of court, Megna asked her how she liked working at "that place near Appleton." She

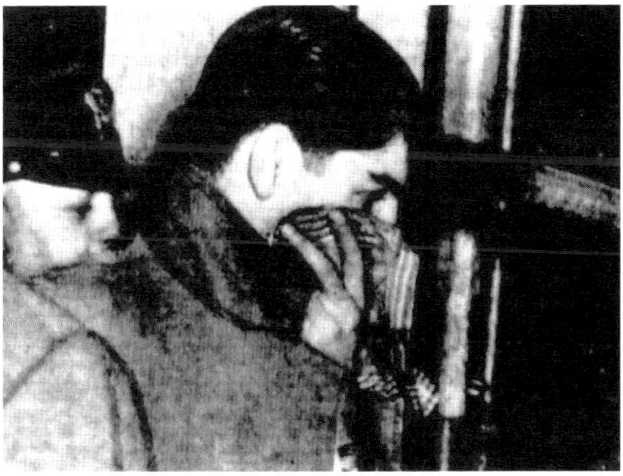

Mobster Louis Fazio hiding his face from the press in a 1946 image. *Author's collection.*

said she had no idea what he was talking about, to which he replied, "Now, Trista, cut out acting dumb. I am Machi's friend as well as his lawyer. What one Dago knows, we all know." Unknown to her, both Machi and Megna were members of the local Mafia. Judge Schinz would later testify that Megna was the woman's attorney at no fewer than five hearings.

Machi and Trista were soon back at Megna's law office, where Machi said that Trista could go back to work at the Blazing Stump in order to pay off the fifty-dollar lawyer fee. She at first declined, and by June she had a quarrel with Machi, so he handed her over to Louis Fazio to be her new pimp. Fazio brought her back to Megna's office, and the two Italians conversed in a language Trista could not understand. Then Fazio said, "I'm going now. You stay with Megna and he'll take care of you."

The attorney concurred, telling her, "So you're without a man now. Fazio told me to talk you into letting me be your man. You can tell all the boys and girls you're with Megna, and they won't bother you. I don't want money; I'm just doing it as a favor."

The claim of not wanting money soon proved to be a lie. Megna took Trista to a resort on Okauchee Lake and spoke to the owner about negotiating a sale on the property. After a price was set, Megna told Trista that if she worked for him for three months, he could afford the down payment, and he could have the whole cost paid off if she kept hooking for two years.

Attorney Megna had Trista working as a prostitute at the Blazing Stump in June and July 1941. One morning at 4:00 a.m., Megna stopped by and Mabel Simonds, the owner, gave him (rather than Trista) $100 that she had earned for her services. On July 6, Megna brought a fifteen-year-old girl from Stevens Point to the Blazing Stump to see Trista. On the ride there, they were joined by Louis Fazio and Nick Gentile. Fazio allegedly punched the girl on the chin during the ride. The girl later testified, "Mike didn't do anything but encourage me. He asked me how I like the racket and when I said I didn't like it and was forced into it, he said, 'Well, you're getting a lot of money out of it, aren't you?'"

Fazio would be arrested for pandering and rape in September 1941, and after fleeing to Chicago and being caught, he was sentenced to two to ten years in Waupun by Judge Henry Hughes of Oshkosh. Fazio also supplied girls to the Blazing Stump and the Tin Roof (a "men's sporting club") at the corner of County PP and South Street in Plymouth.

On October 18, 1941, Gentile and Machi were arrested at their bar, the Gay Spot in Milwaukee, for supplying girls to four houses of prostitution: Joy's Lunch of DePere, Egan's Riverside Tavern of Sheboygan Falls, Club Royal of Plymouth and the Blazing Stump of Appleton. They were accused of being suppliers between October 6, 1940, and June 6, 1941.

Nick Gentile, through attorney James Sammarco, pled guilty on November 5 to aiding and abetting prostitution by putting a twenty-year-old woman in a house of ill repute. Sammarco said, "The defendant did not profit personally. He was just a 'good fellow.' What he did was done as a favor. He was a victim of circumstances. While ignorance of the law is no excuse, we are pleading it here since Gentile knew no better. He is a sick man." Even the sheriff who arrested Gentile agreed that he was probably just a "flunkey" and not the actual pimp in this case. Judge Harvey Neelen sentenced Gentile to a year in the house of correction.

Attorney Mario Megna was on trial on Wednesday, December 17, 1941. He repeatedly referred to his accuser as a "liar" and accused her of committing perjury. Megna's brother John had to tell Mario to relax. Mario said he had not met the prostitute known as Trista prior to May 26, when he had represented her and Nick Machi in court on a disorderly conduct charge. He later represented her in a court case where she attempted to get custody of her eighteen-month-old son. He testified, "She called me to the Gay Spot on June 12 and asked me if she could visit the kid at the dependent home. I took her there. I told her that if she ever wanted the kid she had to prove to the court that she had a good job. And I told her to get out of the racket." Megna said he never took any money from her nor was he ever paid for his legal services.

Megna was convicted of aiding and abetting prostitution on December 18 and faced sentencing the same day. Prior to the sentence coming down, a "parade" of character witnesses testified on Megna's behalf. His brother John, who was also an attorney and Mario's law partner, pleaded with the judge that a conviction could mean disbarment and the loss of a man's livelihood. John suggested that, instead, Mario voluntarily give up his license and move to California with his new bride of only one month. During a recess, Mario was heard to say to the prosecutor, "What do you want to do to me, kill me altogether?" The prosecutor replied, "Well, we're not fighting this case with powder puffs, you know. I want to tell you, I intend to prosecute these cases to the limit." Ultimately, the judge was unimpressed by the character witnesses; Mario was fined $200 and ordered to serve thirty days in the house of correction.

After the sentence came down, defense attorney Charles Swidler approached the judge and made an impassioned speech: "Character isn't something you can put on and take off like an overcoat. Character must be built up through the years. Don't you realize our whole defense was presented today?" The judge struck back, pointing out that one of their so-called character witnesses, Anthony Joseph "Shinebox" Montella, had once himself been convicted of aiding and abetting prostitution.

Nicholas Machi was convicted of pandering on January 6, 1942. He was sentenced to five years in Waupun State Prison by Judge Henry P. Hughes.

On December 30, 1942, Governor Julius Heil commuted Louis Fazio's prison sentence to two to four years, though Fazio had only served about nine months. Heil called the original sentence "excessive." The governor said that, at the earliest, Fazio should not be paroled until he recovered from syphilis. Women's groups protested that this would put other Milwaukee girls at risk, and the original prosecutor believed that compared to other pandering cases, Fazio's sentence was already light, especially given the age of the girl.

Nicholas Machi died in August 1956 in Rockford, aged forty-two. Mario Megna followed his brother's advice and moved to San Jose, California, and died in May 1957 at age fifty. Louis Fazio was arrested for the murder of a mob-connected burglar in Kenosha in 1945, later paroled and eventually murdered in 1972 (he was fifty-eight). Nick Gentile lived until September 1979, dying at age sixty-four.

Interestingly, two of these men would later factor into affairs involving the Fox Cities. Fazio, when seeking a pardon from the governor, enlisted the help of Appleton attorney Mark Catlin, who was also a state representative. You may recall Catlin from the Wenzel Kabat pardon and epilogue. During Fazio's pardon attempts, a scandal came to light in which Catlin was allegedly accepting bribes from Fazio's brothers in order to get favorable treatment. During that investigation, the case of Kabat also came up as being possibly

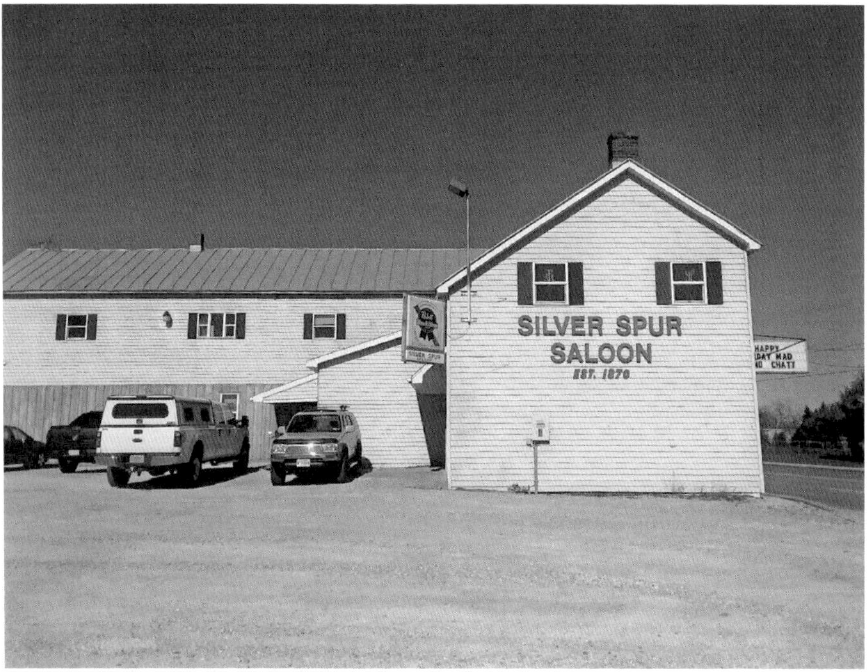

There is a widespread belief that the Silver Spur (as seen in 2017) is the same building as the Blazing Stump. *Author's collection.*

improper. The legal issues that ensued could easily fill a chapter of their own, and readers are encouraged to investigate the matter further.

Gentile was in the Fox Cities in the early 1960s, attempting to open a restaurant on College Avenue with prominent Mafia member August Maniaci (who would later be gunned down in an alley). The purchase and licensing were moving forward, despite both men's long criminal records, until Gentile made a mistake. While in town negotiating the restaurant deal, he became intoxicated at the Siesta Club tavern in Menasha and physically assaulted the owner, Richard Schaefer. The City of Appleton was willing to overlook past criminal offenses (including counterfeiting and the abovementioned prostitution) but was particularly incensed when this new criminal act occurred. The restaurant never opened, creating a setback for the Mafia's move into the Fox Cities.

The Mafia did not rest there, later getting mixed up in another bribery scandal, this time with the mayor of Menasha. But this, like the story of Catlin, is a detour and a story for another time.

9

THE APPLETON BUTCHER

On Monday, September 25, 1967, four children—in first and second grade at St. Joseph Catholic School, 202 South Elm Street—found an unusual package on their playground. It was a brown paper sack, which the children were kicking around the alley and throwing at each other. They played a short game of hockey, whacking the package around the playground. The principal, Sister Illuminata, confiscated the bag and looked inside. When opened, the principal found five dismembered toes and part of a foot. She immediately called the police. Around 12:09 p.m., two officers arrived at the convent, where Sister Illuminata had moved the bag, and they confirmed that the mass of flesh indeed looked like a human foot.

Officers brought the package to St. Elizabeth Hospital, where it was examined by Dr. James Erchul, the pathologist. All the parts were determined to be from the right foot of a human, probably male. Erchul concluded that, although there was a slight odor of decay, because no maggots were present, this was most likely a very recently deceased person, or at least a recent amputation. Sergeant Thiel of the Appleton Police Department speculated that perhaps the foot had come from a nearby hospital and was left outside by some freak accident. Erchul found this unlikely; while admitting anything was possible, he pointed out that most amputated parts are gangrenous—this foot was not. In that case, it would be cremated. Or, in some situations, the part would immediately be turned over to an undertaker to be placed in a grave so the limb would be near the body at a later date.

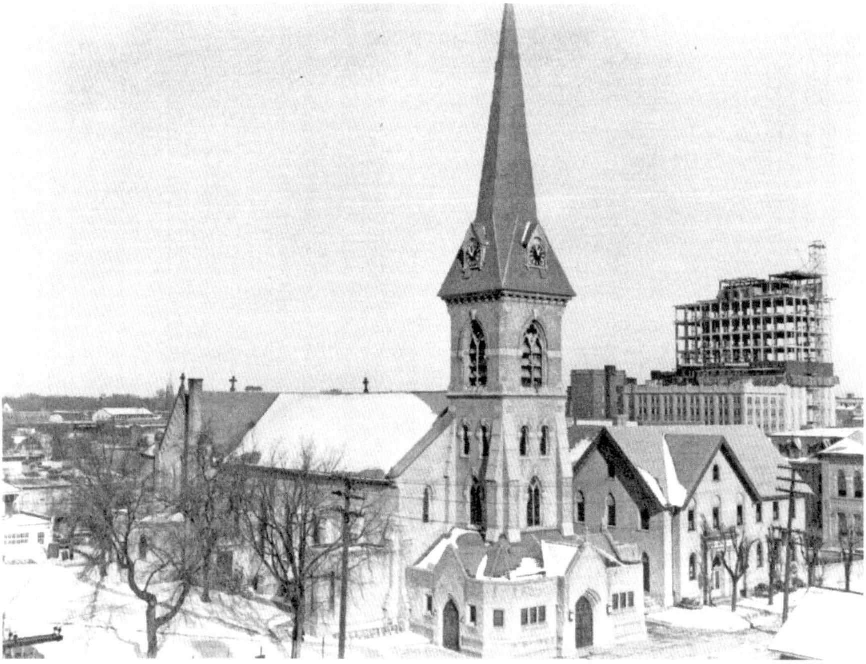

St. Joseph's Catholic Church, where the first human remains were found. *Appleton Public Library*.

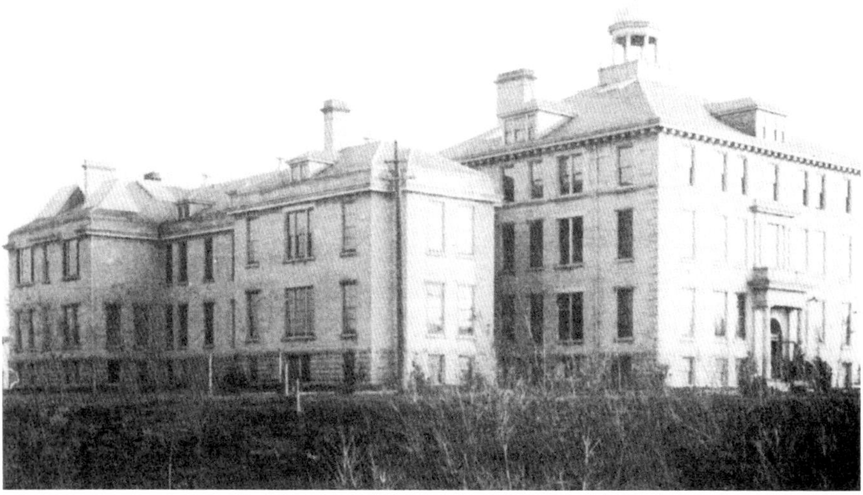

St. Elizabeth Hospital, which has grown and expanded considerably since the time of this photo. *Appleton Public Library*.

In the middle of Erchul's examination, two more packages were brought in that had been found by customer Ernest Stark in LaVern Mullen's ravine next to Koepke's Restaurant. Officers had not yet opened them but, based on the smell, assumed these were more of the same. Their assumptions proved correct; one bag had a left buttock with a wart on it, with part of the pelvic bone still inside. The other had a human liver already beginning to decompose. Upon opening the bag, flies flew out, and those present had to stop and spray the room before they could continue. A closer look revealed a piece of flesh, possibly the navel, attached to the liver and a lack of gallbladder. This suggested the person had the gallbladder removed by surgery, though under the circumstances it could have been removed in other ways. All the parts found were locked up in the morgue refrigerator, where only Dr. Erchul held a key.

By the end of the day, still another package was found, this time a leg bone wrapped in wax paper rather than a brown paper bag. Erchul could only say it was a leg bone, probably a femur, and noted that it had been carefully

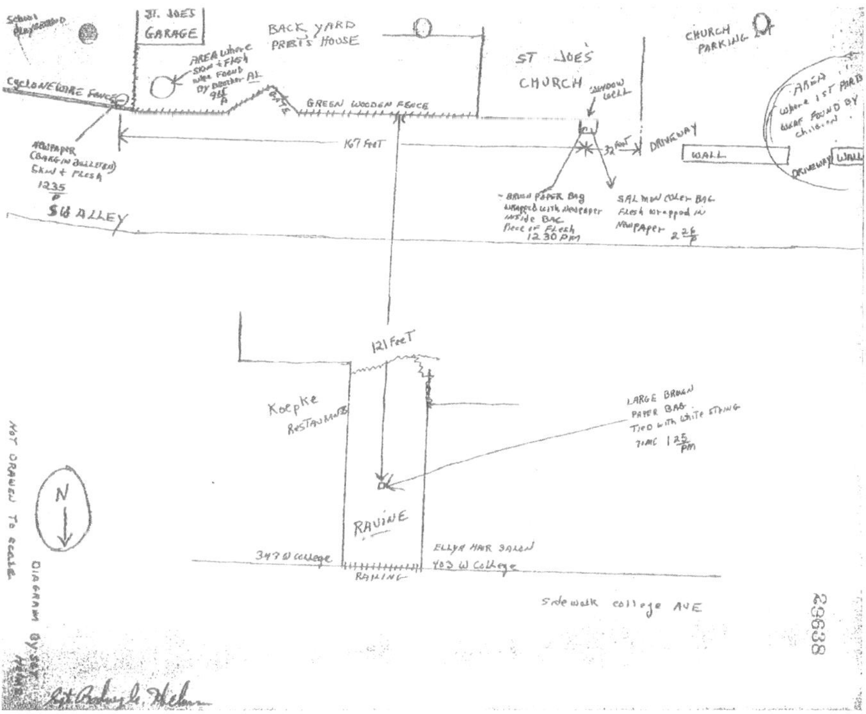

A police sketch showing where body parts were found near St. Joseph's Catholic Church. *Appleton Police Department.*

cut by a sharp instrument. Maggot eggs were present on the bone. The first clues to the perpetrator were also found: a hunting knife and a pair of prison pants belonging to a man named Busch were in an alley near the Appleton State Bank. Stains on the pants appeared to be blood. Did this ex-convict kill a man and carve him into little pieces?

On the morning of September 26, officers led by Lieutenant Robert H. Frailing wore their oldest clothes and proceeded to the Mackville dump. They had received a tip that driver Robert Kappell had picked up trash in the area of St. Joseph's recently and brought it to Mackville. In all likelihood, the trash would already be burned, as a man was on site burning the garbage almost every night. However, the officers were lucky and, while wading through refuse, were able to find a small assortment of bones. Questioning of Kappell revealed nothing unusual during his route and no suspicious characters lurking in alleys.

Just before midnight on September 26, police were called to the North Division Street residence of Sandra Taves in the vicinity of Arbutus Park regarding a disturbance. She told officers she had been having trouble with neighborhood kids, specifically with a man named Howard Skenandore, a known prowler in the neighborhood. Although the disturbance could not be found, police did find yet another package of newspaper tied up with a nylon cord. Upon opening it at the hospital, they found a roughly four-inch piece of flesh from the leg of a man with the bone removed. Another package was soon found nearby containing human ribs with some flesh still attached.

Around the same time, another officer was dispatched to Dag's Drive-In at 1309 East Wisconsin Avenue, where a suspicious shoebox was found. Inside was a hunk of flesh so large it could only have been a section of buttock. Although Detective Huebner thought it might be from a cow or pig, he brought it to the morgue just to be safe. Toxicologist John Liseen and Alan Wilmimosky by this time had X-rayed and examined the liver and found what they believed to be remnants of a shotgun pellet inside. (These names are taken from the police report and appear to be misspelled.) The body parts by now were believed to be from an elderly man, though it was not definite without a head or hands.

The pattern repeated itself again and again as more packages showed up. A length of bone was found in shallow dirt, and a package of flesh was dumped just outside of 403 North Clark Street. Who was behind this disturbing spree?

The case was accidentally broken wide open when Appleton police officer Darrell R. Berglund arrived at the George Schmidt residence, 319 North

Division Street, on the afternoon of Wednesday, September 27. Berglund had previously visited the house on September 15, responding to reports of a fight. At that time, Marie Schmidt asked officers to remove her husband, George. When they informed her that they could not, she asked them to leave. The September 27 visit was merely a routine follow-up, but it soon became much more.

When Marie answered the door, Berglund asked where her husband was. She said that approximately a week prior, a woman had stopped by the house and picked him up to bring him to Milwaukee, and he had not yet returned. She claimed not to know the woman and did not know or care if her husband was in the hospital, an asylum or anywhere else. When asked if she expected her husband to return, she said, "I don't care if he never does." At that point, she asked the officer to leave.

Berglund thought the incident suspicious, so he went to the apartment above the Schmidt residence, where Godfrey Belair lived. Belair considered his neighbors "odd" but got along with them well enough. He did tell Berglund that he had not seen Mr. Schmidt for about one month and had not heard him through the floor for approximately ten days. At that time, he heard a great deal of groaning but decided against investigating further. Belair did tell Berglund that Mrs. Schmidt had asked to use the Belair incinerator; she had her own, but the Belairs' was bigger.

Reporting the Belair conversation back to his superiors, Berglund initiated a chain of events. Chief Earl Wolff contacted District Attorney Nick Schaefer, who in turn called an emergency court session with Judge Keller. At 11:50 p.m. on September 27, Keller signed a search warrant to be executed immediately.

Officers arrived at the Schmidt residence shortly after midnight. No one answered the door, so the police accessed the basement through the Belairs' entryway. Upon entering the house, they found Marie Schmidt sitting in the dark basement, a noose dangling near her head. She appeared to be in shock, almost unconscious, and was brought to St. Elizabeth Hospital and put under police guard in room 417. Within an hour, more body parts were unearthed in her backyard garden. Police believed they belonged to George, eighty-three. The police worked throughout the night, with only a sliver of a moon and flashlights to guide them. Although the temperature dropped to thirty-seven degrees, the officers were working hard enough to sweat in their T-shirts. More than twenty different parts were found, each wrapped in either newspaper or burlap. The stench was unbearable.

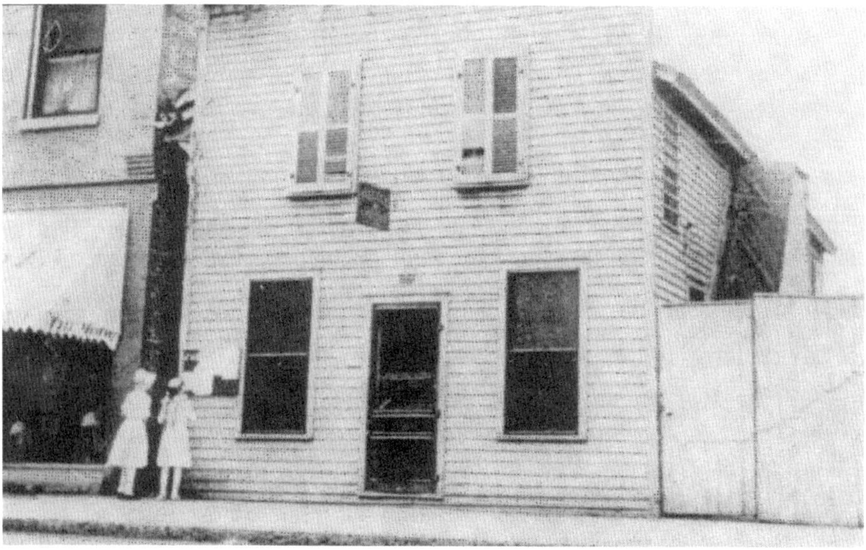

One of the earliest incarnations of the Appleton Police Department. *Appleton Public Library.*

Each body part was put in its own plastic bag for evidence, and the bags were piled into an old wash basin. The garden itself was poorly maintained, containing only dead plants and rotting tomatoes. Throughout the night, neighbors in bathrobes listened to the hum of the generators powering the searchlights and stood in shock as each new piece was scooped up. At 3:15 a.m., the police stopped to talk with reporter Bill Knutson, and still some pieces remained unaccounted for. Most striking, there was still no sign of George's head…until 4:20 p.m. the next day, when it was found in a box under a bush outside of the *Post-Crescent* office.

More than any other part of the body, George's head had experienced great trauma. Officers noted that it was "pulverized extensively" and "the entire top of the skull was cracked wide open." The face was still recognizable, though the forehead had multiple lacerations and the right eye was pushed into the flesh. Only six teeth remained, though this was possibly normal.

At the hospital, Marie was looked after by Dr. Keith M. Keane, head of the psychiatric wing. Dr. Keane informed the police that he would be acting as sort of an "ad hoc" attorney for his patient. He wasn't going to allow an officer to question her until she was considered healthy, and anything she told him (Keane) would be protected by doctor-patient confidentiality, so he wouldn't be passing any information along other than to comment on her general state of health.

Marie's mental state put the investigation in limbo. Until she was able to clear up the loose ends, coroner Bernard Kemps refused to sign George's death certificate. The district attorney also did not wish to file any charges. He was unsure whether or not this was a murder. Clearly, some crime had been committed—abuse of a corpse and disorderly conduct, at the least—but was Mrs. Schmidt even mentally sound enough to stand trial? A records check by the hospital led them to believe that neither Marie nor George had ever been to a hospital or a dentist in their lives.

The Belair family was put up in a hotel for the next several nights, and Godfrey spoke to the media from his hotel room. "Schmidt looked bad," he said. "His health had been gradually failing for the past year or so. One thing I can say—we are sure glad this is all over with and they have found her and someone else is not running around loose."

Belair said they would be moving "as soon as we can."

Another neighbor, Verna Price, remarked, "Who would think anything like this would ever happen in Appleton?"

As of September 29, the police were still not allowed to speak with Marie, but Detective Leo J. Bosch stopped by the hospital room to gather her clothes. She began to speak, and he told her that he was an officer and she didn't need to say anything. She told him she knew who he was and just wanted to know if her dog was okay at the Humane Society. "That dog is alright, but he was getting as goofy as George," she told Bosch. That same day, a call came in from Loretta Black LaMaide at the Salvation Army, who informed police that all of George Schmidt's clothing—including his underwear—had been donated approximately two weeks prior. This suggested an approximate date of death.

On the afternoon of September 29, Judge Gustave J. Keller held court to examine the search warrant and list of items returned with it. Reporter Bill Knudson was present, as was James Bethke of radio station WHBY. Keller ordered the search warrant findings to remain secret until Mrs. Schmidt was charged with a crime. Bethke objected, citing a statute declaring that all search warrant returns are public record. Keller said he would not change his mind, so Bethke informed him that his employer might file an appeal. Upon conferring with his boss, however, Bethke dropped the idea of an appeal. The results of the search warrant remain secret to this day.

The police stopped back at the Schmidt home on October 2 in an attempt to find any prescription medication that Marie might need. None was found, reinforcing the idea that she had never been to a doctor's office before. During the search, they did find a folder marked "For my Funeral." Inside, a note read, "Dear George: Please get this wright. When I am death you get a private funeral for me. I want no church, no prist, and no flowers. I do not want anybody to look at me. Good luck and goodby." Another note read, "George, you take the social security, you can live goot. And take care of the dogs, Heity and Ricky. You take out of the house what ever you want. The television, TV, the radio to. Rent you a emty room and take you a bed and dresser. Don't forget to put paper on the flore for the dog." (Spelling from the originals.)

When searching for a living relative of George's, the only person the police could find was Laura Kate Ellen Grimmer, his sister. She seemed to be as cut off from society as he was and did not know her birth date other than that she was around eighty. Grimmer speculated that George had died a natural death and the unusual disposal method was merely a way to save money. By sheer coincidence, the last time Grimmer stopped by the Schmidt residence was a few hours before police executed their search warrant; the house was dark with the TV on, and no one answered the door at the time. Although Grimmer remembered that George and Marie were married in Crown Point, Indiana, about thirty years prior, she could not recall if her brother had ever been married before that or if he had any children. She knew that Marie had two grown sons.

Grimmer did not know what George's hair looked like, because he always wore a hat. She knew he had never seen a doctor or dentist and was missing some of his teeth. As far as his faith, he was "Evangelical United Brethren Lutheran," but she doubted if he had actually attended a church in many years. She was not able to add anything further. Later that day, Grimmer's son-in-law Charles F. McCoy called the police and volunteered that the Schmidts used to have a boarder named James Sackett who might be more knowledgeable.

By the afternoon of October 2, preliminary autopsy results had come in. Dan Dowd of the state crime lab was able to determine that the body was dead at the time it was dismembered. However, he said an examination of the heart did not show any reason that George would have died a natural death; foul play was still possible. Sergeant Thiel noted in his report, "Dr. Erchul will have to be called in to interpret the report as it is all in medical language. The common layman cannot read it."

Still more stories of unusual behavior started coming in. Peter Kessell called the police to say his daughter and three of her friends were walking by the Schmidt residence not long before when Marie came out and threw candy bars at them. The kids were grateful for the candy but were admonished by their parents for taking treats from strangers. Louis Zaglauer came forward and said he used to be friends with George Schmidt but that they had a falling out some years earlier. However, because they lived in the same neighborhood, they still spoke. Recently, he had said hello to Marie, and she reacted by turning around and exposing her backside to him. Lawrence Behrendt didn't know Marie but said George would always tip his paperboy son and was very kind. Still another neighbor, who was unidentified, said Marie took pleasure in finding fault in others and was not above using foul language.

The most disturbing story of all came out on October 4, when Shirley Vandenberg and Susan VandenHeuvel, both eighteen, spoke with the police. While apartment hunting, they accidentally went to the wrong house and ended up at the Schmidt residence. They asked Marie if they could use the phone, and she told them they could if they were quick, because her husband was very ill. While using the telephone, they observed an elderly man propped up in a chair and covered in a blanket. He was quite pale and was giving off a terrible smell. Initially, they tried to ignore the man, but when news reports started coming out about the house, they realized they had seen a corpse disguised as a sick man.

On the morning of October 6, Lieutenant Frailing and Detective Bosch were finally given permission to speak with Marie in room 417 of the hospital. She now had a new story to tell. The last time she saw George, allegedly, was when she came home from shopping and saw him trying to hit their dog Whitey with a walking stick. She took the stick away and asked him to leave. When asked if she ever hurt him, she did admit to pushing him down the stairs one time. When asked what George died of, Marie claimed not to know he was dead but said the cause of death would probably be "craziness." Frailing told Marie bluntly, "We don't completely believe everything that you have told us….To be very honest about it, Mrs. Schmidt, we know where your husband is. We have found most of him, in fact all of him. A great deal of him was in your garden." Marie denied killing her husband or putting him in the garden. She denied digging holes in the garden. "I am afraid you did," Frailing informed her. "Because some people saw you. Why don't you tell us about it? It would be a lot easier." Marie continued to deny the whole thing, especially digging holes.

When asked what saw she used to cut George up, Marie retorted, "Why do you ask me? Maybe you did it."

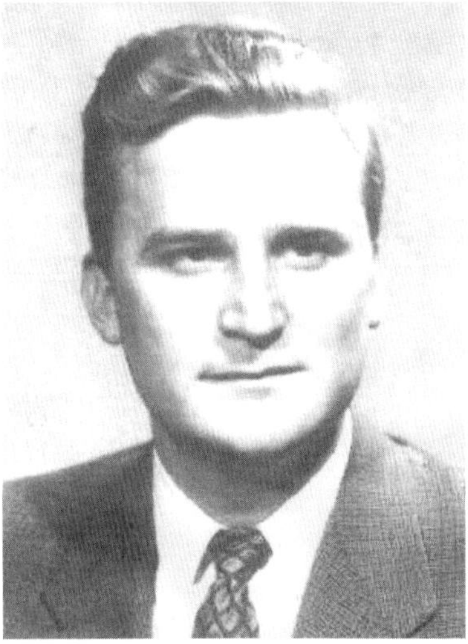

Attorney Donald Jury helped the McCoy family in the aftermath of George Schmidt's passing. *Author's collection.*

She was told that "skin and meat" was found on a saw and she "wasn't fooling anyone" if she thought it got there by itself. Detective Bosch clarified, "The stuff we found on the saw is not a part of your dog."

By October 10, almost two weeks after the initial search, Marie's two sons had still not come to visit her or help put affairs in order. Instead, attorney Donald Lewis Jury assisted Charles McCoy in getting a guardianship for sixty days. He was less concerned with Marie's well-being than with getting a funeral for George. While there was no real hurry (an open casket would be out of the question), the McCoys were hoping to lay George to rest and start getting this family nightmare behind them.

The Maleika brothers, Herman and Walter, finally called the Appleton Police Department on October 14 to check on their mother's health and to see if she had been charged. They were living in Florida and declined to come to Appleton. Walter expressed reservations about getting caught up in a media frenzy, and Herman had a checkered past that left him with unhappy memories—he had served a few years in Waupun for armed robbery and had almost been deported. They did want it on record, however, that if their mother died, they had a will she had written out in 1952. But until that day, they had no intentions of attending to her at the hospital or in a courtroom.

The story began with a bang but quickly reached an anticlimactic whimper on the morning of October 23. In one courtroom hearing, the property of George and Marie Schmidt was given over to the McCoy family, including roughly $6,000 in spare change and small bills found in the house. One-half hour later, a second hearing before Judge Urban VanSusteren decided the issue of Marie's sanity. Not surprisingly, she was determined to be mentally ill, and the judge had her committed to the Winnebago State Hospital (she was later transferred to Outagamie).

George's body was released by the coroner on October 25 and was transported to Ballhorn Funeral Chapels in Sheboygan for cremation. A year and a half later, on St. Valentine's Day 1969, Marie quietly passed on. She had been living at the Outagamie County Hospital (the asylum). Coroner Bernie Kemps called the state crime lab and had it dispose of any evidence it had remaining; although prosecution had always been unlikely, it was now impossible. In the summer of 1969, the Schmidt home (and surrounding buildings) was razed to make way for the new Appleton Post Office.

The Maleika brothers lived out their lives near Jacksonville, Florida, never once returning to Appleton to visit their mother. Esther McCoy, George's niece, continued living in the Fox Cities until her passing in 2002. At the time of this writing, the schoolchildren who found the first remains, as well as the two young women who used Marie's telephone, are all alive and well.

Fifty years later, the story of the "Appleton Butcher" still resonates with residents. Memories are sometimes faulty, or the legends that grow around such events become bigger than the reality. But in this case, whatever people may think happened, the truth is perhaps stranger than fiction. Appleton and the Fox Cities will likely never see such a grisly and macabre event again.

APPENDIX

As of June 4, 1906, there were one hundred men whose names were drawn for a possible position on the Wenzel Kabat jury. While the following men did not make it to the actual trial, it may be of historical interest to know that they were chosen.

J.M. Wissmann, Appleton; J.E. Leach, Hortonia; Jacob Kober, Appleton; Myron Greeley, Ellington; Joseph Stadler, Seymour; Joseph Moyer, Dale; R.E. Rohan, Buchanan; John A. Kilsdonk, Little Chute; Edward Maurer, Appleton; Ernest Gruel, Grand Chute; J.O. Berhhauring, Hortonville; Joseph Dietzler Jr., Kaukauna; Otto Wolter, Appleton; W.S. Halliday, Appleton; H.E. Thompson, Kaukauna; L.H. Hurlburt, Maine; H.J. Prosser, Seymour; I.B. Johnson, Kaukauna; William Leiby, Dale; William Detter, Kaukauna; Edward Jacquot, Hortonville; James Griffin, Bovina; John Flanagan, Maple Creek; Clark Wilcox, Ellington; John Taggart, Kaukauna; Herman Greinke, Appleton; James F. Driessen, Kaukauna; D.G. Stowe, Appleton; A.G. McKee, Black Creek; E.D. Bacon, Dale; Herman Schiegel, Appleton; Charles Reinich, New London; J.W. Cotter, Appleton; C.A. Pardee, Appleton; John Dilday, Center; Edward J. Cance, Bovina; August Klitze, Grand Chute; Matthew Schmidt, Appleton; P.M. Coffey, Freedom; P.J. Sorenson, Appleton; James G. Pfell, Appleton; Fred Reinke, Welcome; Henry Wendt, Osborn; Peter Green, Freedom; Allen Barker, Ellington; A.E. Davis, Appleton; T.W. Armstrong, Kaukauna; E.C. Smith, Deer Creek; John Moriarty, Deer Creek; Frank Solar, Kaukauna; John Tennessen,

Buchanan; Conrad Milhaupt, Appleton; A.S. Galpin, Appleton; Henry Lamers, Vandenbroek; Fred Stacker, Center; Ira Merritt, Appleton; W.R. Bates, Appleton; Jacob Friend, Seymour; Arnold Vanderloop, Vandenbroek; Mike Magaurn, Black Creek; John Pieper, New London; Chris Schroeder, Center; Henry VanZeeland, Buchanan; D.M. Gardner, Appleton; Melvin Raught, Kaukauna; John Ralph, Kaukauna; E.N. Johnson, Appleton; Thomas McNish, Black Creek; R.T. Davison, Liberty; Adoplh Lockschmidt, Greenville; F.C. Witte, Seymour; George Larkins, Seymour; Henry Drephal, Cicero; L.F. Sanborn, Appleton; John C. Ryan, Appleton; A.L. Hamblin, Appleton; Steve Wolfram, Appleton; Anton Stringle, Appleton; George Weyenberg, Vandenbroek; J.G. Fechter, Kaukauna; H.A. Shannon, Appleton; H.L. Mills, Greenville; William Gough, Maple Creek; A.P. Bayorgeon, Kaukauna; Anton Koenke, Appleton; Fred Schultz, Hortonia; Peter Schug, Appleton; Fred Jepson, Deer Creek; J.C. Mitchell, Kaukauna; Nick Dorr, Appleton; Anton Zickler, Appleton; Jerry Callahan, Appleton; John Segeling, Buchanan; John F. Rose, Appleton; S.A. Poole, Maine; Albert Vandenberg, Little Chute; John Schuh, Hortonia; Alfred Mueller, Seymour; W.F. Montgomery, Appleton.

ABOUT THE AUTHOR

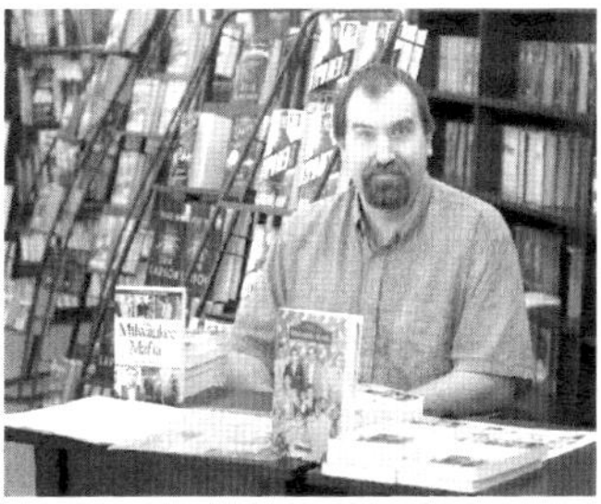

Gavin Schmitt was born, raised and resides in the Fox Cities. Although he earned a degree in philosophy from the University of Wisconsin–Green Bay, the lack of "philosophers wanted" in the local paper had him turn to his second love, history.

Schmitt has written seven books, equally divided between local history and the history of crime in Wisconsin. How do you equally divide an odd number? Because the book you hold in your hands has both of these pursuits dovetailed into one volume. Prior to adding "author" to his résumé, Schmitt was a columnist for a local newspaper, specializing in foreign policy.

Regarded as the foremost expert on organized crime ("the Mafia") in Wisconsin, Schmitt has been interviewed by various newspapers, as well as local, state and national radio programs. When not actively researching (which is rare), he enjoys a strong cup of coffee and watching obscure horror films.